SHARING LIFE, SHARING MOMENTS

An Autobiography

By

Craig Woodard, Sr.

America Star Books
Frederick, Maryland

© 2015 by Craig Woodard, Sr.

All rights reserved. No part of this book may be reproduced, stored in a retrieval system or transmitted in any form or by any means without the prior written permission of the publishers, except by a reviewer who may quote brief passages in a review to be printed in a newspaper, magazine or journal.

First printing

America Star Books has allowed this work to remain exactly as the author intended, verbatim, without editorial input.

Softcover 9781634487139
PUBLISHED BY AMERICA STAR BOOKS, LLLP
www.americastarbooks.pub
Frederick, Maryland

Contents

Foreword 5

Early Years 6
    Early Years Key Points 20
The Move 21
    The Move Key Points 39
College Years 40
    College Years Key Points 53
My Career 54
    My Career Key Points 64
The Divorce 65
    The Divorce Key Points 69
Fighting for Custody 70
    Fighting for Custody Key Points 91
Marrying My Best Friend 92
    Marrying My Best Friend Key Points 103
Junior's Journey 104
    Junior's Journey Key Points 114

Acknowledgments 116
Dedication 121

Foreword

ALMOST TWENTY YEARS AGO I was invited to speak at an athletic function at my High School, Mercyhurst Prep in Erie, PA. I decided to share some of the moments in my life in order to motivate or encourage aspiring athletes. I wanted to let them know that if I could become successful, they could as well. My wonderful High School English teacher, Kathy Pirrello, heard me speak. After the ceremony was over, she came up to me and told me how inspiring my story was. She told me that I should write a book someday and share my story with the world. I never in my life thought that I would write a book. After another twenty years passed and more life experiences, I knew that it was time for me to share my life and share my moments.

Have you ever thought about your purpose on this earth? When I was a child, I thought about that many times. When I got older I tried to make a difference in people's lives. I have always wanted to touch someone's heart with a story that I shared or a loan that I was able to approve at work. I still think about my purpose on this earth, but as I grew older I found my answer. My purpose it to be the best person that I can be while being a good husband, father and son. My purpose is also to provide for and protect my family, as well as motivate my employees to be the best they can be. Along this journey, I have found that the best gift that I can give to people is honesty and letting them into my world. The objective of this book is to inspire you, motivate you and educate you based on my experiences. This is my story!

<u>Early Years</u>

MY NAME IS CRAIG WOODARD, SR. and I was born in Flint, Michigan on June 26, 1974. My parents are Charles (Chick) & Sylvia (Be') Woodard. Prior to my existence, my parents were trying to start a family and my mother was having complications sustaining a successful pregnancy. The Doctor at that time told her that she was unable to become pregnant after a number of miscarriages and disappointments. This was a tough time for them, as you can imagine, considering my Mom was 23 and my Dad was 27 years old. They were ready to have kids. My Dad worked at Highmark Blue Cross and Blue Shield while he was attending Michigan University earning his Doctorate Degree. My Mom was a bank teller at a local bank and they were living in Ann Arbor, Michigan at the time. They kept their faith in the Lord and decided to explore other options.

They thought long and hard about adoption. This was a tough decision and the issue of not being able to have children could play a toll on anyone's marriage. However, my parents stuck together during this time and were 100% on board for adopting a child that deserved to have a good life and two wonderful and caring parents. The process for adoption, back in the mid 70's wasn't anything like it is now, but it was a tedious process to say the least. The phone rang one day and they were told that they were approved for adoption and my older sister Andrea (Angie) Michelle Woodard became their first child. Angie was born in Detroit, Michigan on September 28, 1972 and they were able to adopt her when she was only a few months old. Angie brought a lot of happiness to my parents as they felt that their family had just begun.

Despite what the Doctor told them, the Lord had bigger plans ahead. News that my folks had been waiting to here for a very long time. In the fall of 1973, the Doctor told them that they were pregnant. Of course this brought joy and nervousness at the same time. They had a brand new adopted child and now found out that they are going to give birth to their first child. What a range of emotions. As I said, my Mom had a series of miscarriages before, so they were extremely nervous about this pregnancy. The entire time, they kept their faith. Then it happened, stop the press. On June 26, 1974 I was born via cesarean section at St. Joseph's Hospital. My parents struggled financially at the time. My Mom had to stop working during her pregnancy so they lived off of my Father's income. He worked hard to provide for them while finishing up his PHD. When my Dad earned his degree, he moved the family back to Pennsylvania. They located in a small town called Meadville. My Dad got a job at Allegheny College as the Associate Dean of Student Affairs and my Mom worked as an LPN at Meadville Medical Center.

I remember living in Meadville as a little boy. My sister and me attended Calvary Baptist Christian Academy. I remember always being the only black kid in my class. That experience was very tough for me. The only way I knew how to fit in was to be the center of attention. I was always making people laugh and goofing off. I thought if these other kids laughed at what I did, they would like me. I was too young to realize that they weren't laughing with me, but they were laughing at me. I constantly got into trouble at school on a regular basis. I was always in the principal's office due to being sent there by my teachers. My parents were at the school constantly because of my behavior. That was the first time I realized that there was a difference in races. I was different, I looked different, I sounded different, and I was treated different. It was an eye opening experience for me. This was my life. I had no black teachers, no black classmates and I was just realizing in 2nd grade how differently the world was for me. I remember as a 2nd grader, walking home with my sister and we were getting ready to walk past a white lady who was coming towards us on the sidewalk. I strictly remember her moving her purse from her left arm to her right arm just before we passed her on her left side. I was in 2nd grade and I still remember this. I thought to myself, why did that lady do that? I didn't get it. This was just a small example of what was yet to come as I continued to get older.

At this time my parents started to have marital issues and they decided to separate and get a divorce. They took my sister and I out to dinner one night and gently told us what was going to happen. They both told us very clearly that this was not our fault and had nothing to do with us. They didn't want us to blame ourselves, like so many kids do. They also decided that it would be best if I live with my father and Angie live with my mother. When the separation finally took place, Angie and I were at both of their homes all of the time. It was kind of nice for a little while until my Dad accepted the Dean of Student Affairs position at Coppin State College in Baltimore, Maryland. This meant I had to move with him and leave my Mom and Sister. For additional support, my Mom decided to go back to Nursing School to become a Registered Nurse so she moved in with my Grandparents who resided in Erie, Pa. My Dad was now a single parent as well as my Mom. Most of the time when we hear about being a single parent we think of women who do this all of the time, but I have to give credit to my Father and all of the Dad's out there that take on this task and do it so well. My Dad took great care of me. It was him and me. We did everything together. My dad used to work out all of the time and I would be right there next to him. We moved to Baltimore, MD back in 1983 and we used to go jogging all over the place. I remember him and me driving downtown and going to the Inner Harbor on Saturday's with the windows down listening to music. We would buy Birch Beer and have Bacon Double Cheeseburgers and we would walk around outside for the longest time. He used to take me outside and pitch the whiffle ball to me and let me hit the ball as I worked on my hand/eye coordination. We would go to the basketball court constantly and he was in his 30's at the time and would play pickup games with teenagers and would crush them. I would just sit and watch. He was my Dad. He used to cook and clean and I used to help as much as I could, but even though he had a busy schedule, he always made time for me. I never forgot that. He showed me affection. He shared stories with me. I recall him telling me that he rarely heard his father tell him that he loved him. My Dad told me he loved me all of the time. He would hug and kiss me and make me promise never to feel too old to hug and kiss him back. I'm affectionate with my Father, my Uncles, and my kids as well as my good friends to this day. I've always wore my heart on my sleeve and show true love to people. I learned that from my Dad.

I was going into the 3rd grade when we moved to Baltimore and then he married my Stepmother Jean Wiant. We moved into an apartment complex on W. Cold Spring Lane. It was right around the corner from a Women's college called Notre Dame of Maryland University. I attended Roland Park Elementary/Middle School and it was a huge school. The school had Kindergarten through 8th grade. It was a very diverse school back in 1982. I met a ton of new friends there and I fit in. I went to school with kids that looked like me, sounded like me, acted like me and I felt at home. I even had my first black teacher. This experience let me see life from a different perspective than what I was used to. I saw many things go on in this school. I saw fights all of the time whether it was in the morning before school, during school in the hallways, at lunch, or even after school. I saw some of the older kids smoking outside and I even saw two 8th graders having sex underneath the steps in the back of the school. I was stunned, but at that age I really didn't know what was going on. I was in the afterschool program since my Dad didn't get off of work until 5:00. He would then come and pick me up and I would tell him about my day. My Dad and my Stepmother Jean Wiant sat me down one day and they told me that they were going to have a baby. I was the younger brother so I was very excited to know that I would now be an older brother. I couldn't wait. Nine months to me felt like forever, but the day finally came. Early in the morning on April 5, 1984 they woke me up and said that Jean was having the baby. They got me up and we got in the car around 2:00 in the morning. I remember my Dad dropped me off at my friend Oliver Boyd's house. I had my book bag and a blanket and Oliver agreed to take me to school with him that day. I went inside and snuggled up on the couch and fell right back to sleep. That morning we were dropped off at school and there was an announcement around 8:00. The school secretary said, "We want to congratulate Craig Woodard today." His little sister Ashley Jean Woodard was born at 7:04 this morning." All of my friends started clapping and I had the biggest smile on my face. My Dad picked me up from the after school program that evening and took me straight to the hospital. She was born at GBMC which is the Great Baltimore Medical Center. I still remember that name. I got to hold my sister and feed her that day. It was so special.

Time went on and later that year I did something I will never ever do again in my life. Around Christmas time, early December 1984, there was a holiday special coming on TV that night. My Dad had to go out of town for a meeting and would not be home until after midnight. I asked him if I could stay up later in order to watch the cartoon special. It was one of those Charlie Brown Christmas specials or something like that. You know the ones that come on every year? Well anyways, he said "Yes." However he never told my Stepmom that it was okay for me to stay up until 8:30. My bedtime was at 8:00 during the week. I was so excited to see this special on TV. I couldn't wait. I was sitting in the living room and 8:00 came around and I put the special on TV and Jean came into the living room and said, "Craig it's bedtime." I said "No, Dad said I could stay up and watch this show." She said, "No, he never told me that, so it's bedtime." I immediately got upset and defensive. I said, "No he said I could watch it." She kept telling me to come on and go to bed. Let me explain one thing about the Woodard's, we are very stubborn. VERY! So I said, " I'm not going to bed until 8:30 since he said I could stay up," and I sat right there. She turned the TV off and told me to get in the bed. I said, "NO." She then came over and grabbed my arm and started to guide me to the bedroom. I then put up some resistance. I kept saying "NO," and I gave her the dead weight. You guys know what I'm talking about right? I just went limp and made it harder for her to pull me. She finally pulled me into my room and sat me on the bed. Remember I was only in 3rd grade. I said, "Well I'll sit here, but I'm not going to bed until 8:30 because that's what Dad said." Okay this next part was a life changer for me. Jean then reached down in a quick manner and snatched my glasses off of my face. My natural reaction was to hit her since I THOUGHT she was hitting me in the face. However, she wasn't. She took my glasses off and, yes, I hit her in the arm. Oh NO! What did I just do? She put my glasses on my dresser and walked out of my room and turned the light out without saying one word. I pulled the covers up to my chin and said the same words that you all would say if you were in my position. "MY DAD IS GOING TO KILL ME WHEN HE GETS HOME!" I then shut my eyes and tried to think happy thoughts as I fell into a deep coma like sleep. Just when my sleep was getting good to me I heard my door open. Remember, I'm asleep and everything seemed like it was going in slow motion. I couldn't wake up. I then saw the redness from the back of my eyelids. I now know that the light switch has been flicked on! I still can't wake up. Uh oh! I hear footsteps stomping closer to my bed and for the life of me I still can't open my eyes. All of a sudden the covers were thrown off of me and my eyes opened wide. OH DAMN! It's my Father! Fear came over my body and my mind. I realized what I had done and thought I was going to die. My Dad had the belt, he stripped me down to my underwear and he began to whoop me from the bed all the way to the kitchen at 1:00 in the morning. In between hits I kept hearing him say, "You will never ever place your hands on a female again in your life." He said it over and over again. Then I heard a whimper in his voice while he was yelling at me. I was crying worse than I ever had in my life, but I heard him start to cry. He told me that his Father, my Grandfather, in his earlier years used to be an alcoholic and he used to abuse my Grandmother. My Dad then picked me up off the floor and held me tight and we cried for about 20 minutes together. He told me about how I would grow up to become big and strong and said that I would be able to do some physical damage to others someday. He stressed that I had to promise him that I would never put my hands on a female ever again. I promised him that day and I have held true to my promise. Of course at eight years old, I didn't have a true understanding of what just occurred, but I did know that I had never seen my Father that upset at me before. He tore my butt up and now looking back on the situation, I'm grateful for what he taught me and how he handled the situation. I saw how important this was to him based on his experiences as a child and what he saw his Mom go through. My Father made it clear to me that hitting women would be unacceptable. I idolized my Dad as kid and I still do to this day, so the impact that this whoopin had on me impacted my life immensely.

The following year my Dad wanted to move us a little closer to his job so we moved on the outskirts of Baltimore to Randallstown, Maryland to another apartment complex. I was now going to my 3rd school in a three year period. I was entering 4th grade at Hernwood Elementary. I had to make new friends now and as usual I did. I made friends pretty easily. On the first day of school all of the kids were at the bus stop and I was there with my friend Jay Smith. Jay told me about this bully named Mark Marshall who was in 6th grade who always picked on everyone at the bus stop and in school. Jay was a lot smaller than me so he was an easy target. All of a sudden this husky tall white kid came up to Jay and me and he started pushing Jay around. Jay kept saying, "Leave me alone." He pushed Jay two or three more times and I had enough. I then said to this bully, "Stop pushing him." Mark looked at me and said, "Then I will push you. You're the new kid on the block." So he pushed me once. I told him to stop pushing me. He pushed me again. I told him one last time to keep his hands off of me and Jay and he pushed me to the ground. I stood up and swung at him. I punched him one time and connected with his face. I hit him square in the eye and blood shot everywhere. All of the kids, who never came to our defense, started shouting. They couldn't believe what they just saw after being bullied for so long. This kid ran home bleeding everywhere and everyone said I was going to get into trouble. The bus came, we got on it and went to school. Now this is the first day of school at a brand new school, folks. I got to school and went to my homeroom and I got called down to the principal's office. The principal sat me down and said he spoke with this kid's mother and saw the damage that I caused to his eye. He said this kid has blurred vision and had to get stitches and due to my aggressive behavior he was suspending me from school for three days. I couldn't believe it. He never got my side of the story, never spoke to anyone else who was at the bus stop that witnessed the altercation, he just made a judgment call based on the result of my actions. This school happened to be a predominately White school with only a few African Americans. I started to see how race was playing a part in this situation. The only thing I could think of at that time was to call my Dad. The principal let me contact my Father and I told him exactly what happened. My Dad then left work and drove to the school. My Father sat in the office with me and the principal and began to breakdown the scenario to the principal. He said to the principal, "Are you telling me that my Son is being suspended because of the extent of injury caused to this kid by defending himself?" The principal really didn't know how to answer that question. My Dad always taught me never to start a fight, but don't let someone put their hands on me. It's okay to defend yourself. I didn't think I did anything wrong. My Dad said, "This kid is in 6th grade and from what I have been told he is much bigger than my Son who is in 4th grade. If this kid injured my Son and my Son still fought back causing no damage to the other child, would you still be suspending my Son?" The principal answered "NO." My Dad then said, "So this kid started the fight, my son gave him three separate warnings to leave him alone and my Son defended himself with one punch and he is now considered the aggressor?" He said, "You need to make the disciplinary action decision based on the intention and not the result". I thought that my Dad was my hero and he came to defend me. What a great point. I remember it like it was yesterday. The principal then changed his tune and said, "Dr. Woodard you are right. I jumped to conclusion on this and I apologize. The other kid should be the one that is suspended for starting the fight, but Craig needs to be disciplined for hitting the other student. My Dad agreed. I was given after school suspension that day and then my punishment was over with. The lesson I learned from this experience was to never start any fights or pick on other people. I learned how wrong bullying was and how that made me and those that were bullied feel. I made a vow never to bully anyone and to never let anyone around me get bullied. I also learned that it's okay to defend yourself. I never started any fights in my life, but I ended a ton of them. This gave me confidence and shaped me into a strong minded individual who will always stand up for what I think is the right thing. Dad, thank you for having my back!

At the end of the school year another opportunity came up for my Dad. He was offered another job becoming the Vice President of Student Affairs at Indiana University Northwest located in Gary, Indiana. We had to move yet again. School number four in four years. We moved to a town outside of Gary called Merrillville, Indiana. I was going into 5th grade and I attended Longfellow Elementary located in Calumet, Indiana. In 1985 Gary, Indiana had one of the highest homicide rates in the country. We lived in another apartment complex and I quickly made some new friends. It was tough leaving my friends behind as I moved around, but I took it along with our lifestyle. We moved, that's just what we did and I was starting to get used to it. However, I became friends with a kid named Antoine Perry. He and I were inseparable. Wherever he was, I was and vice versa. We had the same interests, loved basketball, we were Pittsburgh Steeler fans and we loved to swim. Every day we hung out with one another. He and I used to play basketball for hours. We always played with the older kids so that we could get better. This was the time in my life that I started to notice my athletic ability. When the basketball net was ripped down or the chain nets were broken we grabbed a basketball and left the apartment complex and walked the neighborhood as we looked for a house that had a hoop. We went to the door and asked them if it was okay for us to shoot on their hoop. Mostly everyone said, "Yes." We were denied a few times, though. That's how bad we wanted to play basketball. Michael Jordan had just come into the NBA and I loved Michael Jordan. Walter Payton and the Chicago Bears had just won the Super Bowl and he was my favorite football player and the reason why I wore #34.

One day we left the apartment complex and looked for a hoop to play basketball on. I took my Dad's basketball out of his closet and we started walking the neighborhood. We walked everywhere and each person we asked, who had a hoop at their home, said, "No", to us that day. We walked around for hours. Finally we walked down one block and we looked to the left, and there was a hoop on a garage. The garage was on the left side of the house, but towards the back of the house so there was a long driveway on the left side of the home with a fence to the left of it. Antoine said, "Let's ask if we can play there." I said, "Ok cool." We knocked on the door a few times, but no one came. No one was home. Before we left, Antoine said, "Let's play anyway." I knew it wasn't a good idea, but I went along with it. We went to the left side of the house and walked to the back and began shooting around. We shot for about fifteen minutes and then we turned around and there was a car pulling into the driveway. We froze. We couldn't run anywhere since there was a fence all around us. A white gentleman got out of the car and had this angry look on his face like we did something horribly wrong. Looking back on it today, we did. We were trespassing! He said to us, "What are you little niggers doing on my property?" I looked at Antoine and he looked at me and we said nothing. This guy yelled again and said, "Answer me?" I then replied, "Playing ball." He then said, "Give me that damn ball." I looked at Antoine and he looked at me and I threw the ball to him, like I was told. He said, "Go home and tell your father what you did and bring him back with you, then you'll get your ball back." He then went inside and slammed the door. Oh Damn! He took my Dad's ball. We walked home and tried to think of what we could do to replace it. There was nothing we could do. We had no other ball, we had no money and we were out of luck. I never told my Dad what happened when I got home. I didn't know what his reaction would be. Weeks later he got dressed and was ready to go shoot some hoops and he looked in his closet for his ball. He asked me where it was and I said, "I'm not sure Dad." He went out and bought a new one. YES! I was off the hook. I told him what happened when I became an adult. Let me go back to the racist remark that guy said to us. This let me know that racism was everywhere. This was the 2nd time I was called a nigger by a white person. The 1st time was in 4th grade while I was with my Dad. What a horrible and helpless feeling that was. One Saturday in Baltimore my Dad and me were driving around town. He owned a brand new Toyota Supra. It was a real nice sports car. While we were driving, we had the music playing and all the windows were down and the sunroof was open. A car pulled up next to us on the left hand side and there were five white guys in the car that appeared to be in their twenties. They started screaming at us, "Niggers go home, we're going to kill you", and things like that. My Dad rolled up all of the windows and shut the sunroof. He told me that his first thought was that he had to protect me. He sped up and got on the Beltway where he could go faster with hopes of losing these guys. While on the freeway, he lost them for a minute, but they eventually caught up to us and they were even more upset. I asked my Dad why they were upset with us. He said, "They are upset because we are driving a nice car and we are Black." He kept on driving on the beltway trying to think of where he could go. These guys followed us for about a half hour. They weren't giving up. My Dad was going to go home, but thought that was a bad idea because then they would know where we lived. We were not far from John's Hopkins University and it was about 4:00 in the afternoon, so my Dad figured he could drive there since it might be pretty busy there and people would be walking around campus. That was it. He was done driving and he was ready to stand and protect me. He pulled into this parking lot and the guys pulled up next to him. He said to me, "Craig whatever happens to me, you stay in this car and keep the door locked until help arrives." I said, "No Dad, I want to get out with you." He said, "No. Stay in the car and DO NOT OPEN THE DOOR". I began to cry. He got out of the car and grabbed a stick from underneath the seat that he always carried for protection. He locked the door and he said, "If y'all want some, come and get some because I'm not running anymore and I will NOT let you touch my Son. You are going to have to KILL ME!" I cried a little more after hearing that. There were five big guys against my Dad. He stood his ground and he knew if he was going to go down, he was going to go down fighting to save my life. These guys saw the look on my Dad's face and they knew that they messed with the wrong person. All of the education and professionalism that exuded my father had gone out the window. You can take the man out the hood, but you can't take the hood out the man! That saying is so true! My Dad meant business and they saw it clearly. They all got back in the car and said, "You are lucky this time." Then they drove off. My Dad was going to give his life for me. He was going to fight to keep me safe by any means necessary. He was and will always be my hero. He got back into the car and began to teach me about life and about what I would face being black. He explained to me that he didn't want me to hate white people for what those guys did to us. He told me that if I hated the entire race of white folks then I would be just as bad and ignorant as them. At nine years old, that made total sense to me. He told me that he wanted me to love people, but to be aware of who I kept around me. He told me that I would face situations like this throughout my life and how I choose to handle the situation would shape what the outcome would be. I also saw how my Dad would give his life to save mine. This experience has resonated with me all of my life and has taught me the first job of being father, PROTECTING HIS FAMILY. This would come into play later on in the chapter when I wrote about custody.

On a lighter note, tryouts for the basketball team were approaching and this was going to be the first year that I would play an organized sport. I was so excited. I went to the tryout and I made the team. My Father, being in higher education, was very particular about grades and sports. It was simple. If I didn't have good grades I didn't play. Well after making the team our report cards came out and I had two D's. Needless to say, my Dad took me off the Basketball team just as quick as I made the team. This hurt me so bad because I loved playing basketball. I cried for a few days. I didn't see it then, but of course I see it as an adult now. The most important thing at that time in my life was to get a good education and as a part of my discipline, the thing I loved the most was taken from me in order to prove that. I got my grades up and only played in 2 games that season. Let's recap. 2nd, 3rd, 4th, and 5th grade were all spent at different schools. Four schools in four years. My Father didn't want me to go through all of these changes any longer especially in an area like Gary, Indiana. He wanted to give me a hometown. He wanted me to develop some lifelong friends and give me more stability. Therefore, he and my Mom came to a mutual agreement on sending me to Erie, Pa to live with her and my older sister. I missed my Mom, but I knew I would miss my Dad and my little sister Ashley. Having said that, they still believed that this was the best thing for me at the time.

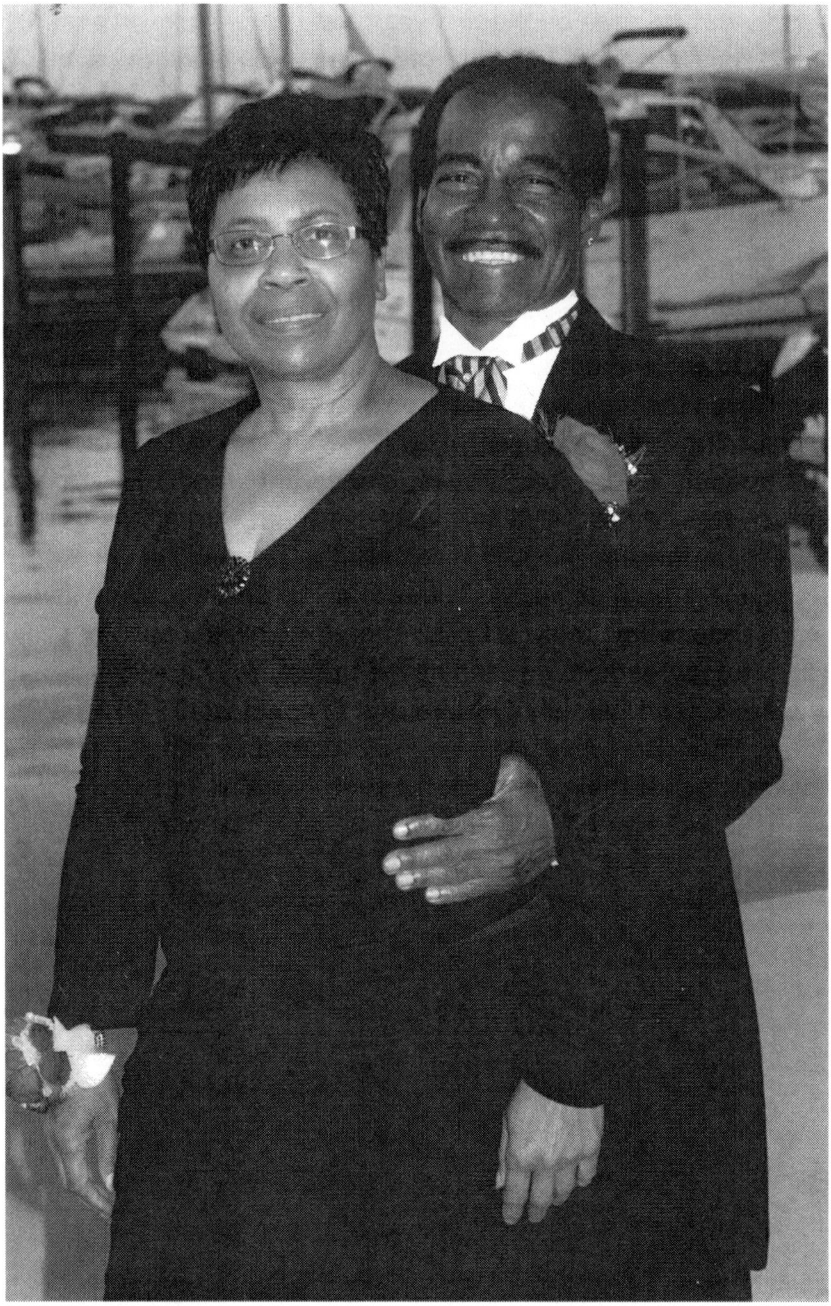

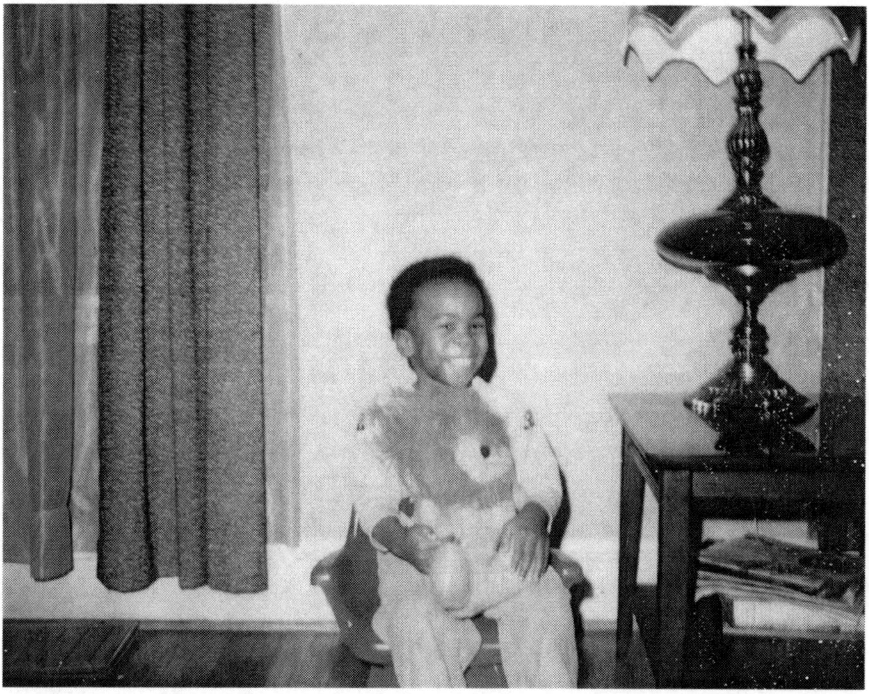

Early Years Key Points

- Children please realize that there is a struggle growing up in a single parent household.

- Be patient and know that your Mom or Dad is doing the best that they can.

- Always remember that if your parents get divorced, kids it is not your fault. Do not blame yourself.

- Bullying will always be wrong. Don't stand for it and don't participate in it.

- Always defend yourself. Never start any fights, but it is your right to protect yourself.

- Know that racism still exists. Handle yourselves accordingly. Violence is not the answer.

- Portray yourself in a positive light so that others don't target you for no reason at all. Don't give the police an opportunity to categorize you by what you choose to wear or how you choose to wear it.

- Always hold yourselves with an Executive Stature.

The Move

IN THE SUMMER OF 1985, I moved to Erie, Pa. with my Mom and my Sister Angie. We went to school at St. Patrick Elementary. I started my 6th grade year there and this was the first Catholic School that I attended. I remember my Dad coming to visit during Thanksgiving and he pulled me aside and sat me down and had a long talk with me. He asked me if I remembered my friend Antoine Perry. I told him yes of course and I asked why. He said that he was told that Antoine was walking home on the side of the road one night when it just got dark outside and he was right out front of the apartment complex when he was hit by a Semi-Truck and knocked into the ravine. He said the security guard saw it happen, but the truck driver kept going not knowing that he hit him. Antoine got up and said he was okay. He picked up his basketball and the security guard asked if he can call his mother. Antoine told him, "No it's okay. I'm sure I'm okay." The security guard let him walk home. Antoine's Mom always worked the night shift so no one was home when he got there. Apparently he suffered massive head swelling when he went home and he fell asleep on the couch like he usually did. When his Mom arrived home from work the next morning Antoine was dead. I immediately started crying for two reasons. #1 I just found out that I lost one of my good friends and that was one of the first times I lost someone so close to me. #2 had I not moved to Erie, I would have been with Antoine and I could have gotten hit as well and that scared the hell out of me. It hit me how precious life is and that the decisions we make as kids can have a cause and an effect on our lives. We were never supposed to leave the apartment complex and my Dad said he was walking out front of the apartment complex. I know Antoine went to play ball somewhere down the street without permission. My heart still hurts when I think about what happened.

Moving on, my Mom's lifestyle was much different than what I was accustomed to with my Dad. She was truly into her religion and went to church constantly. My Grandfather, Elder Boyd Francis, was the Pastor of our church, so we were there six out of seven days a week. For example, when I was in 7th grade and I played basketball for St. Pat's we would have practice during the week from 6:00 - 8:00 at night. Church service was at 7:00 during the week, so she would come pick me up at 6:50 and I would have to leave practice to go to Church during the week. I never understood why. However, I do give my Mom a lot of credit for raising my Sister and me. She did the best job she knew how. I always knew she loved me very much. She is a very special Woman and I have never met an enemy of hers. Having said that, I had one of the best basketball coaches from 6th grade – 8th grade in the area. Coach John Purvis. He gave me an opportunity to grow athletically and he encouraged me to use my skills whenever I had the opportunity. I was always one of the faster one's on my team and I could jump pretty high as well. In 6th grade I could grab the net on the basketball hoop. In 7th grade I could just tip the bottom of the rim and in June right after I graduated from 8th grade in 1988, I dunked my first basketball at the Mercyhurst Athletic Center. My Aunt Bettie was one of my biggest supporters when I was in grade school. She came to many of my games and cheered loud and proud every time. I had no other family there to see me play, but I could always count on my Aunt coming to support me. Coach Purvis would always get on my case during practice. He was always riding me until one day I asked him why. I said, "Coach why do you always yell at me?" His response was something that stayed with me for the rest of my life. He said, "Woody, I yell at you because you have more athletic ability and talent than you realize you have. I stay on you in order to bring that out of you. Don't be upset when I'm yelling at you. I'm yelling at you because I care. Be upset when I stop yelling at you because that is when I won't care anymore." The light bulb turned on for me when I heard him say that. I worked hard always in practice and took everything he said to heart. This stayed with me through my athletic career. Coach Purvis, thanks for the encouragement. He pulled me aside during our playoff games in Oil City in 8th grade and told me to try to dunk the basketball any chance I got. He said he didn't care if I missed, but the attempt will intimidate the other team. Well I had three opportunities to dunk the basketball in the game against St. George. I missed all three, but everyone at that point knew who I was and what I could do.

In 8th grade I also played football for St. Andrew's for the first time ever. I was a nose guard. I spent time that summer with my Dad, so I was never able to learn any of the offensive plays. I was supposed to be a running back, but we had two good running backs already. I fell in love with the sport. I had an opportunity to go to two different schools. In 1988 you had to take a test and pass it in order to be accepted into Tech Memorial. While in 8th grade I became good friends with Khyl Horton. He played basketball for Wayne Middle School. He was 6'4 and could dunk and was a lefty as well. We used to talk about playing for a State Championship when we got to high school. Both he and I went to Tech Memorial to take the test. During our 8th grade year, there was one Coach that would always come to see us play. He always wore a Green and Yellow Baseball cap with an M on it. His name was Greg Majchrzak. He was the Basketball Coach at Mercyhurst Prep. They showed an interest in having Khyl and me come to the Hurst. We passed the test to get into Tech, but we both decided to go to the Hurst and pursue our dream. I remember going to my Grandmother Woodard's house for dinner on a rainy Sunday and my cousin Earl, who attended MPS, was just leaving. I got in the car with him because he wanted to talk to me. We went for a ride and he said, "Coach Majchrzak wanted me to let you know that he wants you to come to the Hurst. He checked you out all year and wants you to become a Laker." I was excited about that especially when I found out that Khyl was going as well. Then I found out my other friends were going there as well. Shelby Wiley, Jeff Sansom and Chris James. Our freshman year started up at the Hurst and early in the year I met Freddie Jones who transferred in. We had a great time at Mercyhurst Prep.

They didn't have a football team and for me that was depressing, but I wanted to concentrate on school and basketball. I played soccer my freshman year since I led the Parochial league in scoring when I was in 8th grade. It wasn't because I had skills or anything, I just kicked the ball and chased after it. I was faster than the other players so I always would score. I also played it just to stay in shape for basketball season considering all of the running we had to do. I had some good Soccer coaches in my life as well. Walter Soboleski and Al Metrik were two of the soccer coaches I learned a ton from. Two wonderful guys that taught me some great life lessons. Coach Soboleski taught me that no matter what color my skin was, be the best athlete that I can be and any coach will be forced to play me because I was that good. Thanks Coach! Coach Metrik taught me that work ethic is everything. No matter how good you think you are you can always get better. Coach Metrik passed away some years ago, but I hold him close to my heart daily.

The Mercyhurst experience was a different one, but a good one. I have so many memories from High School. There were some good ones and some bad ones. My Mom was a single Mom raising two kids and she graduated years ago from Nursing School at the top of her class. She became a Registered Nurse and worked at St. Vincent Health Center when I was in High School making a minimal annual salary so she really tried to make ends meet. She lived pay check to pay check and there were many times that we had to go without. I remember a number of times when we only would have the butt ends of the bread left and I had to make a sandwich with that for lunch to take to school. The other issue on a few occasions was that we didn't have any sandwich bags in the house, so I would have to wrap my sandwich in a plastic bag that you brought your groceries home with in order to bring my sandwich to school for lunch. It was embarrassing to say the least, but this was my life. Other times if we didn't have any plastic bags, I would get the last piece of aluminum foil to wrap my sandwich in. The problem was that the foil wasn't enough to cover my entire sandwich. I would wrap it up as best as I could and put in in my book bag for lunch. We had hard times often. It was hard for her to afford sneakers for me and as a teenage boy who played sports, I went through sneakers very quickly. She would always say, "Ask your Dad to buy you some new sneakers." At that time I would rather walk around with holes in my shoes than to be questioned by my Dad as to why I needed a new pair, so I would go without. It just seemed easier. At times my Father was very impatient and wasn't the easiest to communicate with after I moved. He didn't call us as often as we would have liked and wasn't able to come to the majority of my games due to him living out of town. I felt like I was missing him in my life and our relationship changed after I moved to live with my Mom. We were very close at one time, but the distance I felt had done something to our relationship. My Mom and I didn't have the best relationship when I was young, but have a fantastic relationship as adults. I felt as if she never supported me, in the way a child looks at being supported. What I mean by that is she never came to any of my soccer, football, basketball games or track and field meets. Athletics is what meant the most to me back in school and to not have her support me athletically truly hurt me. All I wanted was for my Mom to see me play ball. What this did to me was it made me become a tangible person. I started to look at my value or my self worth being measured by the amount of trophies or awards that I won. I didn't have my parents there to say, "Good job Son or you played well Son," so I substituted what I desired to hear from them with the accolades that I have achieved. That is such a deep statement. It wasn't until I was around 36 years old that I was able to put all of my awards away and be okay with it. I liked seeing them, it validated me. This is what I thought, but it truly didn't validate me. It only validated what I did. I validated me, how I turned out validated me, my family validates me. That is what's important to me now.

For those kids that get involved in athletics or any other activity that you may like and you feel like you don't have the support from your parents, I encourage you to speak up. Ask your parents why they won't come. Try to convince them that you need that type of support in your life. There may be some of you that won't get the support you are looking for because your parents are working and preoccupied with something else. Some parents want to be there, but can't be there. It doesn't mean that they don't love you. It simply means that they can't be there physically. Remember that it's not the end of the world and that you are not in this alone. If I made it through that tough time you all can make it as well. My parents never knew this until now, but I will share this with you and them. When I started playing organized sports in 6th grade I used to play with a picture of them in my shoe. It was something I did to help myself feel supported by them. Since my Dad lived out of town and my Mom chose not to come, I wanted to have them with me in every game that I played. I know that this is superstitious or maybe even weird, but even though my parents were not at every single game I played, they were with me at every single game. I never told anyone about this until now.

As I said before, my Mom was and still is a very religious person and I respect that, but in my opinion as a child, she was raising us to live her life and not live our own. I didn't like being in church six days a week. That is one of the reasons why I don't attend church now as an adult. I am confident in my faith and have a solid relationship with God. It was too much when I was in Grade School and High School. My Mom raised us the best she knew how and I love and adore her for that. That was on butt whoopins, tough discipline and going to church. As I continued to get older though, my relationship with my Mom continued to prosper. When I was a freshman at Mercyhurst Prep, my good friend Khyl Horton and I didn't get a chance to play basketball on the same team. Khyl started varsity as a freshman while I played on the freshman team. I had some remarkable moments that Khyl still talks about today to people. I get random text messages from Khyl from time to time when he is out with someone or talking to someone we grew up with and he will say things like "I'm with Rich Bush, please tell him what you did at the JFK?" It's so funny getting random text messages from him because I know he is filling people in on something that he thought was amazing back in the day and that other people didn't know about. Now mind you, he is the one that gave me the nickname "Soop, and that was short for Super Negro." He always thought that I was a great athlete. Well here is the story about the JFK Center. Back in 1990 I was at the JFK Center with a few friends of mine. My cousin Chris James was there, Kevin Carroll, Terrell Maxwell and Lawrence Renshaw. We were in an Anti-Drug Rap Group called the Dope Busters and we were practicing. We took a break and we started playing basketball and I started to dunk a few times. I went down the court at the far end and went up with two hands and dunk the ball as hard as I could. While I was up there I heard a loud crack so I let go of the rim immediately. When I landed I looked up and I shattered the backboard. The glass was falling down right above me so I moved out of the way and everyone was in shock. They went crazy. To shatter a backboard while dunking gave me the ultimate street credibility. It was unbelievable! The first person I thought about sharing this story with was Khyl Horton. I said out loud, "Oh Chief won't believe this". Now of course if it was 2014 we would have recorded it on our smart phones and uploaded it to Facebook or Instagram, but this was back in 1990. We had nothing but our word. Therefore, I took a dollar sized chunk of the backboard and put a piece of white athletic tape on the back of it to keep the glass from falling apart and I wrote the date, time and location on it so that I could show Khyl Horton as proof. I carried this backboard around with me in my Moms car. I stored it in the glove compartment. One day I drove over to Khyl's home and I said, "Come outside, I have to show you something." He came out to the car and I handed it to him. His eyes got wide and he could not believe it. We laughed from a long time that day. Every time he looked at me he just laughed. He said, "Soop, you have mad hops my brotha." That to me was respect from the top player not only in the City, but the top player in the State. Other stories he would have me elaborate on was the fact that I jumped over three different players during three different games when they were setting up to take a charge. This was much like what Vince Carter did during the Olympics when he jumped over the 7-footer. The three individuals that tried to take a charge on me were Greg Tirak at the Strong Vincent Gym, Keith Nies at the Booker T. Washington Center and Jake Delsandro at McDowell's Gym. They were all great players. All of these scenarios were the exact same. I was coming down on a fast break and those guys set up to take a charge and I would jump and spread my legs right over them avoiding all contact and I made all three layups in the process. They stood there expecting me to make contact, but I jumped right over them and the crowd and their coaches couldn't believe it. I get asked about that every once in a while. Great memories! My junior year was definitely a special year for me. During this time I had the peer pressures that most kids have. Whenever I was walking around our neighborhood on 23rd or 24th St. there were always guys that liked to smoke weed and drink. I was always offered weed and alcohol back then, but my Uncle, Roland Francis, eliminated the feeling of ridicule for me. He would always tell people that I didn't smoke or drink because I was an athlete. They respected what he said and left it be. I never felt the pressure to take part in something that I didn't want to do.

At the end of my sophomore year, I was told that Coach Ron Costello was coming over to Mercyhurst to start the football program. I was ready to go. I was the starting running back and played safety as well. We went 8-2 that year and beat Cathedral Prep to win the Metro League Varsity Reserve Championship. What a great experience. Shortly after football season ended, basketball season began. We had a great team and the best team so far in school history. We played in the Double-A division as well as the Metro League. We entered the season with our motto being "Whatever it Takes." We were determined as a team to do whatever it took to win. We worked so hard in practice and the prior summer during workouts and know if we came together we would do something special that year. We lost to Cathedral Prep twice that year and both games were very close. We also lost to McDowell twice as well and to Academy once. The Metro League definitely prepared us for the AA State Playoffs since all three of those teams were AAAA teams. That year in the game we beat Academy, I had my first metro league dunk during the game. I was guarding one of the point guards that night and I stripped the ball from him at the top of the key, took one dribble and threw it down. The sound that I heard after that in the Hammermill Center was unforgettable. I had a few dunks during a game when I was a sophomore (ie: Franklin HS, Dubois HS, Dunkirk HS), but there was a different feel doing it in the Metro League. We went into the playoffs with state title on our minds. We picked off each team we played and got stronger as the playoffs continued. In the semi-quarterfinal game we played at Clarion University a highlight opportunity was created once again. At mid-court I was playing defense against the point guard. He dribbled towards the sideline and I stripped the ball and took off down the court. I took about four dribbles then without even thinking about it. I leaped into the air and dunked the ball hard as I could. I was only 5'9" and that's what impressed so many people including myself. That was one of the best highlights of my basketball career. We won the game and moved on to the Western Final game played at Edinboro University against Kennedy Christian. We lost to them in the District Playoffs so we knew we had our hands full. This game was played on Live TV as well. Another special part of this moment was the fact that our Girls Basketball Team also played in the Western Final game right before we did and they won. The pressure was on us now. What a great game we played. It was close and came down to the end, but we ended up pulling it off, with a trip to Hershey Park on the line, it was MPS over Kennedy Christian for the Western Finals and we earned the right to represent Western Pennsylvania in the PIAA Boys AA-Basketball Championship.

This was such a special feeling. This was the first time in Erie History that both the Boys and Girls Teams from the same school went to Hershey to play for State Championships. The winner of the Eastern Final Game was Wilkes Barre GAR who were no strangers to the State Title Game. The year prior, in 1990, they played the Girard Boys Team led by my buddy Marc Blucas and lost to the Girard Yellow jackets. Their All-State forward, Bobby Sura, was back for his senior year averaging 35 points a game and they were undefeated on the year. The prior year they went undefeated until they lost in the championship game so they played two full seasons and only had one loss on their record. Everyone counted us out going into this game. No one, but our school and our team gave us a chance to win this game. Whatever it takes right? That's what we lived by. We prepared hard for this contest and we had an All-State forward of our own. One of my good friends I spoke about earlier, Khyl (Chief) Horton. Khyl was the Metro League's leading scorer and ironically we were in the position he and I dreamed about in 8th grade. There was a send off for us at the High School the day before the game as many Mercyhurst Prep students and supporters met us and the girl's team up at the Hurst. We took two buses down to Hershey and we wanted to cherish every moment of this experience. Only one team per class gets the opportunity to play in the State Championship each year. We were ready.

We watched the movie Hoosiers all the way down to Hershey. That movie seemed to fit us that year and what we were trying to accomplish. We arrived in Hershey later that day and we were able to take a tour of the Hershey Chocolate Factory. It was a great experience and one I will remember for the rest of my life. We had our fun the night before, but on game day, it was all business. We walked into the gym and this by far was the largest gym we had ever played in. The gymnasium was enormous and very intimidating. However, just like the movie Hoosiers, Coach Majchrzak said to us, "These rims are ten feet just like the rims at home. It's the same so we need to play the same." That made total sense to us. Now it's game time! We came running out with our silk warm up suits on after chanting in the hall way in order to be heard. We hit the floor and the butterflies were present. We couldn't believe we were here, but we knew we earned the right to be. We did our warm ups and had our team huddle. The buzzer sounded in order to start the game. The starters took the floor. Brian Wedzik at the point, Ron Swanson at shooting guard, Khyl Horton at forward and Big Brian Dahlkemper tipped things off at center. I came off the bench into the game as the sixth man about three minutes into the game. We had a huge following as the crowd was packed with green and white. As I entered the game, my assignment was to guard Bob Sura. I was up for the challenge. I scored a quick three-pointer not long after I entered the game and I had a nice layup as well. I drew a charge on Bob Sura on the defensive side of the ball and we had a decent lead at the half.

In the 2nd half Bob Sura and the Wilkes Barre squad had a reminder of what happened the prior year against Girard. They came out and played ball. They made a run late in the game and they thought we would break. Our weapon just got stronger. Khyl Horton came alive and hit bucket after bucket stealing the show. Khyl scored 21 points with some crucial buckets down the stretch and I scored 11 off the bench. We combined for 32 of our 58 points and we held Bob Sura to only 30 points. I say ONLY because Sura averaged 35 points that year. The final score was 58-55 and we brought Mercyhurst Prep home our first ever Boys State Championship. We thought we were sitting on top of the world. We finished the year at 27-5 while Wilkes Barre GAR ended up with a two year overall record of 62-2 losing two straight State Titles to Girard and us. What an awesome feeling. Now of course Sura went on to become a star at Florida State and ended up playing for the Cavs and the Rockets during his professional basketball career. Khyl earned a scholarship to George Mason University. He played there for two years then transferred to Gannon University for his final two. I can always say I held Sura to five points under his average and we won by three along with a State Title. Throughout the playoffs our girls' team played always at the same gym as us and they played before us. Well this time they scheduled us to play first and girls played after us. Our girls had a wonderful squad so now it was time to cheer them on. Our girls' team was led by Teresa Zumigala and Angie Potthoff. They were playing Allentown Central Catholic led by All-State guard Michelle Marciniak. What a game that was. It went back and forth until our ladies ended being too much for ACC and the Mercyhurst Prep Lady Lakers brought home yet another State Title for the Erie area. This was such a special moment. We all rushed the court and celebrated together that night and we all deserved it.

My junior year continued into Track Season. My sophomore year I won the Metro League High Jump Championship clearing 6'2. My junior year I won the Metro League High Jump championship once again. It was a great athletic year for me in 1990 – 1991. My senior year at Mercyhurst Prep, I had high expectations of myself. I worked out hard in the summer preparing for the upcoming football season. We had a tough schedule ahead of us and this was our first year as a Varsity team. Our first Metro League victory came over the East High Warriors. I got a chance to play against my cousin Cliff Crosby, who went on to play for the Colts in the NFL. We were 3-5 entering into our last football game of the season and I was 2nd in the Metro League in rushing behind my friend Mark Tate from Cathedral Prep who also ended playing for the New England Patriots. It was a Friday in school and I was walking down the hallway and Khyl Horton came up to me. Khyl said to me, "Soop, you have your last game tonight and you need to rush for 274 yards in order to reach 1,000 for the year in only nine games. If anyone can do it, it's you Soop!" I said, "Thanks Chief I'm going to play my heart out tonight." During the day I lost one of my contacts and I didn't have a spare pair with me. I didn't have time to go to the eye doctor to get another pair either so I had to play the game at night with only one contact. Khyl said,

"Soop, you are telling me you only have one contact and you are still going to try to set this record?" I said, "I have no other choice." We got on the bus and travelled out to North East as we faced the Grape Pickers. This was a high scoring game and it was a very physical one as well. Ron Costello was the type of Coach that would call a play and if it worked he would run the same play until the other team stopped it. Well my play was forty seven pitch. That was a sweep to the left. Tony Tate was our Quarterback, Gabe Zaczyk was the left halfback, Donnie Fuller was the Fullback and I was the right Halfback. One of my best friends, Jeff Sansom, was the Wide Receiver on the left side so he did a ton of blocking for me as well. Well we were in the 4th quarter and we were losing the game by three touchdowns and we had one last drive. The team started playing hard in order to help me to reach one thousand yards. I already rushed for two hundred yards and scored two touchdowns and we had to go seventy six yards in order for me to score, but seventy four yards for me to reach one thousand yards for the season. Coach kept calling forty seven pitch. Each time I was picking up yards, 8 yards, 3 yards, 10 yards, 5 yards as the clock kept ticking. Coach kept saying same play, same play. Finally we had only three seconds left on the clock and Tony called the play. We were at the line and he said "HIKE." He pitched me the ball and I caught it heading to the left and the offensive line held their blocks and I scored on the sweep diving into the end zone with no time left on the clock and our sidelines rushed the field because WE did it. As a team we accomplished what we set out to do at the beginning of that last drive. I ended up scoring three touchdowns and I rushed for 276 yards in that game which is still a single game school record. That broke the record that I previously set against Brooksville rushing for 236 yards a couple weeks prior. Even though we lost and finished 3-6 that year, we earned respect on the Varsity level. I completed my senior season rushing for 1,002 yards in nine games. I love my teammates. My individual accomplishments came from team effort.

After that season I truly fell in love with the sport of football to the point that I knew I wanted to play football on the Collegiate Level. I had a few visits that year and I was getting recruited by some big schools. I would get letters from Rutgers, the University of Houston, Pitt, West

Point and a few others on a weekly basis. I will have to admit though. If I could do school all over again knowing what I know now, I would be a better student. My grades were not where they should have been and I was passed over by all of the big schools so I scrambled to get into a Division II school. At this time my father had left Savannah State College in Georgia, where Shannon Sharpe played and was the Vice President of Student Affairs at Kutztown University in Kutztown, Pa. That is where NFL Hall of Famer Andre Reed played College ball. I was invited there for a visit along with Mercyhurst, Gannon and Edinboro. I was offered a scholarship at Kutztown and I would have played with John Mobley, who ended up getting drafted as the 16th pick by the Denver Broncos in 1996, but I didn't want to go there and be on the team because of my father's influence. I wanted to make a name for myself. I chose to go to Mercyhurst College instead. That was only two miles away from my Moms house so it was far enough from home and close enough to visit home. The rest of my senior year athletically was a disaster in my eyes. We had more talent on our Basketball team from 1991-1992 then we ever did at Mercyhurst Prep and we were the favorites to win another AA Boys Title. This year Khyl, Shelby Wiley, Freddie Jones and I, along with many others were seniors. Josh DiBello was a junior that year, but we were stacked and ready to go. We played some tough games throughout the season and lost a few close ones, but the main goal we were focused on was winning another State Title. We ended up losing to Kennedy Christian in the District 10 playoffs after one of their guards hit about 8 three-pointers. He couldn't miss that day. We had been there before though. We lost to them in the District 10 playoffs the prior year then beat them in the Western Finals. However this year was a bit different. In the first round of the playoffs we ended up losing with a shot at the buzzer. Just like that our High School Basketball Careers were over. It came and went that fast and we were out of the playoffs. I was so upset that I don't even remember who won the State Title that year nor did I care. Next up for me was Track and Field. See practicing for track and field was very tough to do when we didn't have a track or a field. We would run on West Grandview Blvd, run in the hallways. I could never practice my high jumping form since we didn't have a high jump pit. My Coach would have me take a basketball and go into the gym and practice reverse dunks since that was the closest to the actual high jump motion. What we accomplished was just from raw talent, not practice at all. That year we did some special things. There were two meets that we all got ready for. The Metro Meet, which was all of the city schools competing and the District 10 meet. I took part in many events throughout the season to help my team earn as many points as possible. I ran the hurdles at Fort Leboeuf and I won that race and I had never ran hurdles in my life. I ran the 100m in 10.99 seconds and the 200m in 22.5 seconds. I was a better 200m sprinter than I was a 100m sprinter. I also was the anchor leg in our 4X100m relay. Our team consisted of Chris James, Jeff Sansom, Tony Tate, myself and Darren Jones was our Alternate. During the Metro Meet, Mercyhurst Prep showed the entire city what we were about. Tony Tate won the 100m and 200m dashes and he was named the Cities Most Valuable Track Performer. I won the high Jump title with a jump clearing 6'4" and I won the long jump title as well with a leap of 21' 9". I was named the Cities Most Valuable Field Performer. Our 4X100m relay team also took first place in the city as well. A clean sweep in the major events. However, on my last long jump attempt, even though I had already won with my very first jump, I decided to try to break 22 feet. Both my high jump and long jump results ended up setting new school records since I set them originally and they both remain school records to this day. Looking back on it, I should have just walked away and brought my day to an end, but I felt great that day. My last attempt I was sure was going to be my best jump. The District Meet was only one week away and I was going to be ready. I got focused and blocked everything out. All I saw on the long jump track was the white board and the pit. I knew if I hit the board perfect I could break 22 feet. I started down the run way full speed ahead. My steps felt nice, the wind was at my back, I kept repeating to myself, hit the board, head up and reach. Hit the board, head up and reach. Finally I was at the point of impact. My head was up, but I felt my entire left foot hit the white board. I am going to make the perfect jump. All of this is going through my mind in a split second. I left the ground, my head was still up, I arched my back and hope that momentum carried me as far as it could. I felt my body descending from the air so now it was time to reach as far as I could and I remembered to fall forward not backwards. I landed in the pit and all of a sudden I felt an incredible pain in my right ankle. Oh my goodness. I landed wrong. I landed with my ankle turned in and I stretched every single ligament in my right ankle. I also heard the line judge yell out "FOUL." I thought I hit the white board square in the middle, but my toe was over the line. They measured it anyway and if I had moved back less than half an inch, I would have jumped 23'8". I tried to stand up and I couldn't. What have I done? My ankle is ruined. All I could think about is how my greed could cost me my performance in the District 10 meet in one week. I was on crutches for the next few days until Wednesday. I finally began to run on Thursday, but I wasn't at full speed. I pushed myself as far as I could go during the District Meet, but due to my injury I failed to qualify for the State Championship. Another disappointment. Now it has settled in that my entire High School Athletic Career has come to an end.

But not just yet! I had been voted by the City Coaches to represent Mercyhurst Prep in the 52nd Annual Save an Eye Football Game. I became the first Mercyhurst Prep player to ever play in the Save an Eye game. What an honor. I grew up watching players play in this game. The City vs. County matchup. I made the squad. Who was our Head Coach? Joe Bufalino from Strong Vincent. The Strong Vincent Colonels won the PIAA State Football Championship that year and they had many of their players on the City squad. Mark Tate, who led the Metro League in rushing from Cathedral Prep elected to play in the Big 33 instead of the Save and Eye game so I should have been the featured Running Back since I was 2nd in the league in rushing. Well that's what I thought, but that definitely wasn't the case. Dan Olson was the Quarterback for the City, while Tony Robie and Tim Romanski were the Half Backs. We were running Strong Vincent's offense. The Wing-T it was called. This was a very confusing offense if you are not used to running it. So all of the other guys who played on other City teams had to get used to it. Every year it was the same matchup of talent. The City squad always had speed while the County Team always had size. This year the City had Speed and Size and we were ready to play this game. I had butterflies at the beginning of the game as usual. Veterans Stadium was packed and this was my opportunity to show the entire City what kind of football player I was.

My playing time was limited and the game seemed to look more like the Strong Vincent Colonels against the County team. I only carried the ball twice the entire game. However, I took advantage of my opportunities. The first time I touched the ball I scored on a 54 yard run. It was designed to go off tackle, but I bounced it to the outside on the right and took it up the sidelines. My next carry was in the 2nd half and I picked up 10 yards for the first down. Two carries, 64 yards and one touchdown with an average of 32 yards per carry. Not bad, but that's all that I was given. I was very upset about that until Norman Davis, who lived right up the street from me, pulled me aside and said that he took notice that I ran the ball very well and that I opened the eyes of many in the city. He told me about the politics in sports and told me to just keep playing as hard as I could. That made me feel so much better and I appreciated that pick me up. I walked right down the street to my house at 2502 French St. and sat on the front steps watching all the traffic riding by and at that point it hit me that my High School Athletic Career was now over. What a great way to go out! By the way, we beat the County that year 37-8.

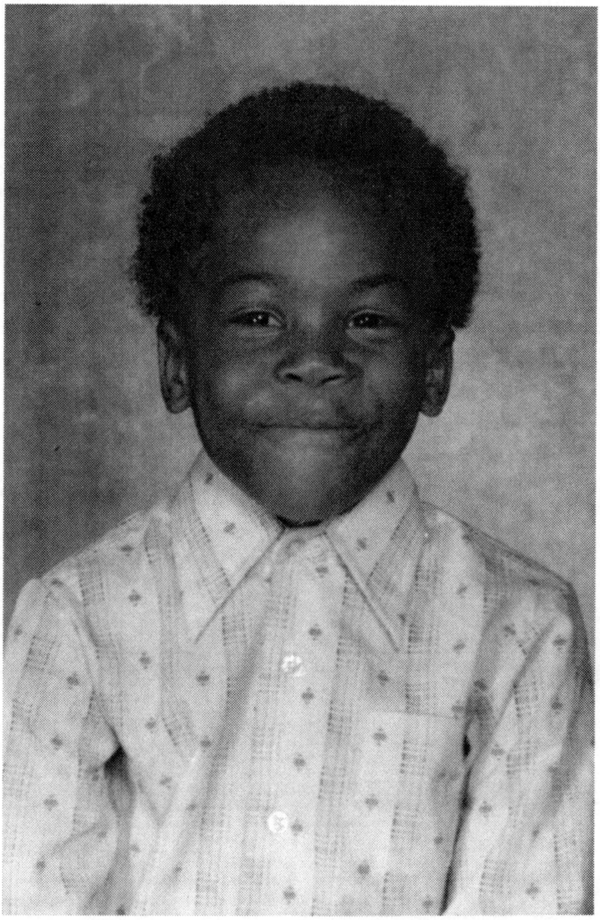

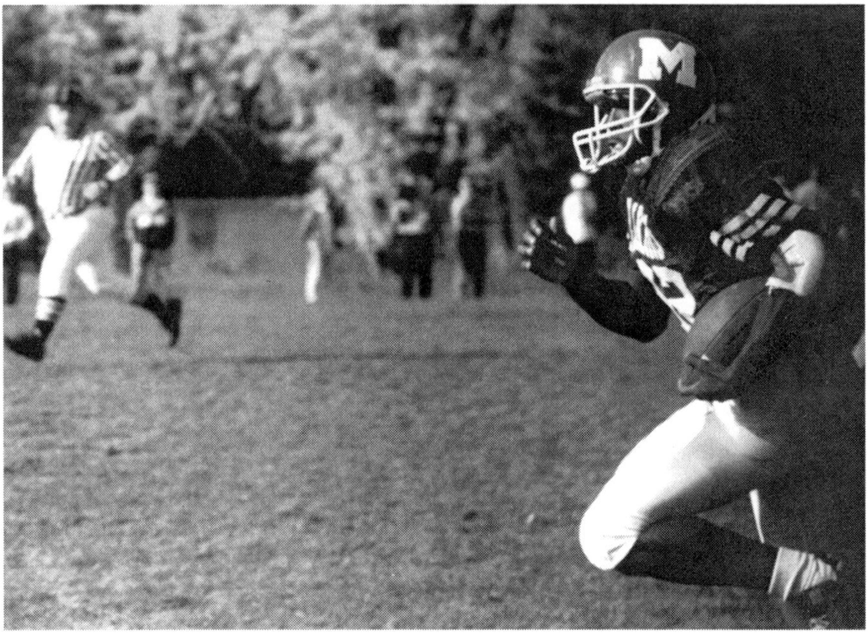

The Move Key Points

- There is going to be change when moving from one parent's household to the others.

- Lifestyle adjustments are going to be challenging, but keep positive communication with your parent so that they know what you are thinking and feeling.

- Be open to change. Being open minded is a great quality to have.

- Single Dad's do just as good of a job as single Mom's do raising children. Father's take pride and be proud of the role that you have chosen.

- Kids get involved in an activity at school or at your local community center.

- Stay away from anyone that can bring negativity into your life. This is not needed and will prevent you from achieving the desired goals you set forth.

- If someone puts peer pressure on you to do something that you don't want to do, remove that person from your inner circle.

- High School education needs to be a priority in your life. Work very hard and take your future seriously.

College Years

MY COLLEGE LIFE STARTED one week after I graduated from High School. I had a meeting with the President of Mercyhurst College in Erie, Pa., Dr. William Garvey, about my acceptance into the school. I was very nervous going into this meeting, but I knew that I just had to be myself since my college career was relying on the outcome of this meeting. I sat in his office and he told me that he was happy that I chose Mercyhurst to pursue my college education. He told me that he reviewed my transcripts and had seen many athletes that had grades like me before and he had seen many of them fail because they felt that sport was the most important thing to them. He shared a story with me that really touched me right before he had me sign an agreement with him. He asked me if I remembered James "Buster" Douglas. I said, "You mean the Heavy Weight Champion of the world who beat Mike Tyson?" He said, "Yes that's him." He asked me if I knew that he was a former Mercyhurst College student. I said, "Really? No I didn't know that Sir." He then proceeded to tell me that years ago Buster Douglas came to Mercyhurst with hopes of playing Basketball. He was only here for the Fall Trimester. I said, "Why only one trimester?" He told me that Buster Douglas couldn't cut it at Mercyhurst when it came down to education. He ended up dropping out of school. He said, "I don't want you to be another Buster Douglas." However he did tell me that he became successful anyway after becoming the Heavy Weight Champion of the World, but the point he was making is that he didn't want to give me this opportunity just to have me throw it away. I heard his message loud and clear. He then gave me a proposal. He stated to me that he wanted to see if I was capable of doing the work that Mercyhurst required. He said he wanted me to take two classes in the summer prior to fall enrollment. He wanted me to take World History and a class in my Major which was going to be Communications. He said if I received a B average in both classes I would be accepted to Main campus and eligible to play football my freshman year. He said if I received a C average I would be accepted to main campus, but not eligible to play football until my sophomore year. He said if I received a D average I would be accepted to Mercyhurst North East and not eligible to play football my freshman year. He then said if I fail both classes, he would do me a favor and pay for the classes and that I would not be accepted to Mercyhurst at all. Keep in mind folks, I just turned 18 years old and I'm having this conversation with the President of Mercyhurst College. I was nervous, but confident in my abilities. An inner city kid from a single parent household has just been challenged. I face challenges all of my life on a daily basis. The only difference here is that this was my future. However, my confidence came out and I told Dr. Garvey that he had a deal and I would make him proud of me. I signed the contract and signed up for my two classes and they started the following week.

I was present at class every single day and I did each one of my assignments. I studied daily, even though it was Summer time, I knew that I had to buckle down and take my school work seriously. Little did I know, Dr. Garvey had a history background. Dr. Allan Belovarac was my Professor for World History, but one day Dr. Belovarac didn't make it to class and in comes Dr. Garvey. He taught the class that day and I was amazed and intimidated at the same time. I always sat at the front of the class and I made sure I took some very good notes. I struggled a bit taking the tests, but I was pulling B's and C's in my history class. I took Television Productions as my second class and that really peaked my interest. After weeks of classes the final grades came out and I earned an A in Television Productions while earning a C in World History. As you now, an A and a C equal a 3.0 or a B average. I was now able to play football for the Hurst my freshman year. A week later Football Camp started. Jim Chapman was our Head Coach. He recruited me along with Coach Armstrong and Coach Curtis. I entered into camp as the 3rd string Running Back. I was determined to get my time on the field, but I knew I had to be patient. I was on the scout team early during camp. For those of you who don't know what the scout team is, it's the 3rd string players on offense that run plays against the starting defense and vice versa. All I remember is All-American Robert Bandish and John Langer on the defensive line running after me yelling my name. I was not going to let these big guys get their hands on me. So I did what I did best. I used my speed and moves to get away. Needless to say, I made it through camp. We now had our first game of the year. Our starting running back was Pat Ott. He was a great guy and I learned a ton from him. He was coming off of a year where he had shoulder surgery. In the first game of the year Pat reinjured his shoulder and was done for the entire year. I now moved from 3rd string to 2nd string. I didn't play in our first game at all. During our second game we played Maryville at Veterans Stadium. That team was from Tennessee. Chris Soltis was now the starting running back and he was a senior just like Ott was. Chris started off running the ball well, but had a tough time hanging onto the ball in the first half as he fumbled 2 or 3 times. Coach Chapman came to me at halftime and said to me, "Woody are you ready?" I told him I was born ready. He said, "Good because you are starting the 2nd half." I got two things, butterflies and a huge smile on my face. We are at home, a block away from my house and I am going to be getting the ball. I couldn't wait. When I was in grade school I used to sit on my steps at night while a game was being played at the Vet and I used to listen to the loud speaker. I still remember listening to a Cathedral Prep game and the announcer saying, "Gary Dance the ball carrier, he picks up 45 yards on the score." It was the greatest thing ever. Now they will be calling my name. Well our announcer, Barry McAndrew, was just inducted into the Mercyhurst University Athletic Hall of Fame in 2014 for his years of service and accomplishments and he had the voice that we all can remember. Back to the game. The 2nd half began and the team had never seen me before. I had to make sure I remembered my assignments on each play. The adrenaline was pumping and so were my legs. I ran around, through and over many players in the 2nd half by leading us back to a victory by rushing for 133 yards and the game winning touchdown. The position was now mine to lose. I couldn't believe that I started 3 weeks ago as the 3rd string Running Back and now I am the starter. My hard work and some unfortunate situations helped me out in this matter. My buddy Chris Soltis changed his position to fullback and he blocked for me the rest of the year. What a great athlete he was. I learned a lot from him and we developed a great bond as teammates.

The following week we played our Cross Town Rivals. Gannon University. It was also homecoming weekend for us. On Friday night Coach Chapman took all of the starters to the Holiday Inn on 18th and State. I asked our Quarterback Chris Logero, who I roomed with that night, why are we staying at a hotel? He said, "Coach doesn't want any of us to get into any trouble or be influenced by all of the festivities going on around campus." Remember, I had just turned 18 years old two and a half months earlier so I didn't know what he's talking about. All I knew is that I needed a good night sleep. We got up in the morning and drove back to campus to eat breakfast and prepare for our 1:00 matchup. The Vet was packed, it was a beautiful sunny day, the temperature was perfect and you could smell football in the air. I was so nervous, but my nerves always went away when I had the ball in my hands. Chris called my number in the huddle in the first quarter, I took the handoff and sprinted up the left side for my first touchdown of the game. I was averaging about 5 yards a carry during the game so we had pretty good ball movement when we wanted to. Late in the 2nd half they called my number again on a counter play and I scored right up the middle. When I hit the end zone for my 2nd touchdown I struck the Heisman Pose. Boy what did I start? Late in the 4th quarter we were on the move, as I said I was picking up about 5 yards per carry. It was 4th and 1 around the 25 yard line and instead of giving the ball to me they decided to use me as a decoy. We ran a QB Keeper after faking the handoff to me and we were stopped short of the 1st down. Gannon ended up winning the game 24-21. I ended the game with 124 yards and two touchdowns.

The following week we played Canisius College out of Buffalo, NY. During the warm ups I had many of their players calling me Heisman because of the pose I did against Gannon. Clearly they saw that game tape and had prepared to shut me down that day. Sometimes your preparation falls short. On the kickoff we got the ball and our returner was brought down at our 6 yard line. Poor field from the start. The offense took the field. I was lined up deep in the end zone in the Tailback position. My number was called 28 pitch was the play. That was me sweeping to the right. Butterflies set in and everything was in slow motion. Logero said, "HIKE," and I took off to the right keeping my eye on the ball. I caught the pitch and hesitate like I'm going to cut to the inside, that set up the stock block on the outside and I saw that so I sprinted to the sideline right around the block. I got to the corner and I turned it up. I made one more cut towards the middle of the field and I was off to the races. 94 yards for the touchdown untouched. 6-0 the Hurst. My teammates Matthew Hatchette, former NFL Wide Receiver, and Dayne Bailey were going crazy! We kicked off to them and had a four and out series and they punted back to us. The offense took the field once again. Guess who was getting the ball? Yep, 29 pitch was called this time. Sweep to the left. This time I took the ball and ran 54 yards and I slipped down at the five yard line. On the very next play I took it in for the touchdown and just like that we were up 14-0. I had three carries, two touchdowns for 153 yards and only five minutes had run off the clock. We won the game and I ended with 222 yards rushing and three touchdowns.

The season continued on and the Heisman name lasted throughout the year. I thought it was funny that the other team picked up on that, but I continued to play as hard as I could each day. We ended up going 5-4-1 that year, but I had a record setting year surprisingly. I set the Freshman Rushing record with 1166 yards, I set the Single Season Rushing record with 1166 yards, I set the Longest Run from Scrimmage record at 94 yards. I had the most 100 yard games in a single season at 5. I had the 2nd highest rushing performance in a game with 222 yards. I was also the first player in school history to rush for over 1,000 in a single season. I was voted the Mercyhurst Offensive Player of the Year and I was named the ECAC Division III Southern Division Rookie of the Year. I was on cloud nine, but I wasn't satisfied. I was 5'10", 185 lbs. and I ran a 4.45 in the 40 yard dash. What could I do to push myself to greatness and get my team to win? That answer came in the off season. In January of 1993 my Grandfather Elder Boyd Francis starting having some heart issues. He went to the hospital and became very sick. He was in the hospital for just about 6 months. I used to go visit him from time to time, any time I could borrow someone's car to drive to St. Vincent, I would pop in and say hi to him. He was so proud of me. He used to brag to all of the nurses when I came in. He would say, "This is my Grandson from Mercyhurst

College. He's the star Running Back." He was so proud of me and I felt that. I grew close to my Grandfather over the next few months. I also knew that I had to get a job. It was that time. I was on my own now. My Aunt Bettie Dickens worked at National Fuel Gas Company and she said they would be hiring someone for the summer. I went to the main office and filled out the application and I got hired. I worked 2nd shift from 3:00 – 11:00. On July 2nd, while I was at work, I received a phone call from my Mom. She told me that my Grandfather wasn't doing very well and he took a turn for the worse. I asked my Boss if I could leave to go see him and he said, "Yes." My Mom came to pick me up and we went straight to the St. Vincent Hospital. When we got there, he was struggling to breathe. I let him know that I was there. He fought hard to stay alive, but the Lord called him home that evening. My Grandmother took his death so hard. That was her best friend. It was a major change for the entire family. It took me a long time to get over his passing.

I started to hit the weight room and run at Veteran Stadium every day. I would walk into the stadium and there were workers there. I asked them if I could work out on the field and one of the guys said yes. I would bring in plastic cups and use them as my markers since the field wasn't lined. I would do cutting drills, run 40 yard dashes and do other drills to improve my explosiveness. When I was almost done, I would go to the bottom of the stairs at the bleachers and run up and down the stairs all around the stadium. After I finished that, I would go to the hill right next door in between State Street and Old French Road and I would run that hill until I got sick. I got my inspiration from Walter Payton. By the end of the summer, I was 5'10", 205 lbs. and still ran a 4.45 in the 40 yard dash, but I added 20 lbs. of muscle. I was ready to ball in 1993. Coach Armstrong came up to me and said, "Woody, are you ready to rush for 1500 yards this year?" I said, "1500? Coach I set my goal on 2,000 yards." He knew I was dead serious. However, we had some changes this year. Coach Jim Chapman left and we got a new Head Coach. His name is Joe Kimball. Coach Kimball came to us from St. Lawrence University out of Canton, New York. He installed a brand new offense. He introduced us to the Veer Option. This was a very difficult offense to run, but this was our main offense. That cut down on the amount of carries that I was going to have. Entering into the 6th game that year, we were playing Duquesne University down in Pittsburgh on their brand new turf field. I wasn't a fan of this type of turf. Turf burn was horrible and I just had a bad feeling about how it didn't have much of a grass feel to it before the game. The first series in the 2nd quarter changed my life forever. We ran a play where I would run to the flats on the right side for a pass. I caught the ball and made a move on the defensive end. I hit the sideline and instead of going out of bounds I saw my wide receiver stock blocking for me and he had great position on the cornerback. To his left I saw nothing but Green land. I decided to stay inbounds and I ran close behind him and planted my right foot in order to cut back towards the middle of the field. At that exact moment, the exact time that I planted my foot, a linebacker from Duquesne hit me on my left side sending my momentum out of bounds. The pressure from me planting my foot and getting hit at the same time twisted my knee as my foot stuck in the turf and I heard a loud snap. I hit the ground and felt an immediate sense of pain. Worse than I had ever felt before in my life. I was going into shock. I realized that I blew my knee out. I tore my (ACL) Anterior Cruciate ligament, tore my (MCL) Medial Collaterial ligament, I tore my Meniscus and I had a bone chip. I totally destroyed my knee and my dream of playing in the NFL. This was one of the worst times in my life. I cried for days after my injury. The doctor was very optimistic about my return, but let me know that I would have to undergo major knee surgery and be on an extensive rehabilitation program to have any chance of playing again.

Before my surgery I was sitting in the rehab room at Mercyhurst and I was icing my knee down. I was sitting in a tub of ice water and after I got past the pain of the ice I began to look at my knee and I started balling like a little baby. I couldn't contain myself. I got myself together then I walked to over to the film room while on crutches and I asked Coach Kimball if I could watch the game film. He let me put it in and left me in the film room by myself. I watched the injury over and over again and I just broke down once more. That was my future out the window right there on the screen. I cried so hard until I felt a hand on my shoulder. I looked up and it was Coach Kimball.

He had tears in his eyes as well and he said, "Woody you will make it through this. You have a strong work ethic and you never quit and I know it may not make sense right now, but this could have been the best thing to ever happen to you." I knew where he was coming from, but I knew it would get worse before it got better. Later that week I had my knee surgery at St. Vincent's Hospital. A great doctor performed my surgery. He used to be the team doctor for the Utah Jazz. I felt that I was in good hands. The surgery went well, but there was a long road to recovery ahead of me. I have to give a special thanks to Gannon University and Coach Tom Herman for allowing me to use the Gannon pool for rehab and I have to say thanks to one of my Athletic Trainers Dave Jaconski for taking me to and putting me through pool therapy twice a week at Gannon University. I had some tough times and depressing moments. I dropped out of one of my classes that I couldn't catch up on. I didn't feel like I was a part of the team anymore. I was working out on my own and I stayed out of the locker room missing workouts with my team. For that act, Coach Kimball sent me a clear message. He called me into the football office and he suspended me from participating in upcoming training camp and I was suspended for the first game of the year. This hit me like a ton of bricks. I didn't feel a part of the team before and I now I could do one of two things. Either quit the team or work harder to earn everyone's respect and fight to get back to my running back position. I chose option number two. When camp began I was there every single day for every single practice. I worked out on the field next to my teammates so that I could get ready for the season and they could see that even though I wasn't allowed to practice with them, I was still out there with them. Three practices a day I was there. I never missed a meeting and I did what I could do. That impressed not only my teammates, but my Coaches as well. I cheered my team on as they played the season opener. I wanted to be on the field so bad. The following week we played on the road at Frostburg St. I got my opportunity to play and when I entered the game everything went through my mind. Could I still play? How will my knee hold up? Do I still have it? Did I lose a step? Well my jitters got the best of me, but I was happy to be on the field. I had a poor performance and we lost the game, but my teammates stuck by me. Before the third game of the year I had another injury occur. After our Sunday work out, Brian Burton and I were walking through Old Main which was one of the buildings on campus. I walked down to two steps right before the door and there was water or some type of liquid spilled all over the steps. My foot slipped on this liquid and I put my hand up to catch myself on the door and my momentum forced my hand to go right through the glass window. I cut an artery in my right hand and I was bleeding everywhere. The guys took me to the car and drove me down the street to Urgi Care, which was located right on 38th and Pine Avenue. The doctor saw me there and said, "You severed an artery and you need major surgery, you need to go to the emergency room now." We got back in the car after he put a towel and some dressing on my hand and they drove me to Hamot Hospital. When I got there they called Coach Kimball and told him what occurred. My Mom was notified as well and they ended up doing Microscopic Surgery on my hand. I suffered nerve ending damage as well so I lost a lot of feeling in my hand. I had to make a decision whether I should take a medical redshirt and sit out that year or keep playing. I called my father and asked him what to do while all along I was wanting him to tell me to redshirt. He told me that this was a decision that I had to make on my own. He said, "If you feel you can play then I won't tell you to sit out." That made my decision tougher. I thought back to all of the blood, sweat and tears I put into strengthening my knee. I had to miss one game due to this surgery, but after that I decided to finish out the year and play. One of my highlights that year was receiving over 100 yards against Gannon University. For some reason I always played well against them. We had a mediocre season to say the least. We finished the year at 3-6-1.

    I now had one season remaining. Going into my senior year I wanted to leave it all on the field. I was 205 lbs. and I may have lost a step from my knee injury, but I felt as good my senior year as I did my freshman year. I was gearing up to be the work horse running the ball. We played some great teams that year and we were the first team to beat Robert Morris on their home field. They were coached by Joe Walton, who played for Pitt back in the 50's, the Redskins and the Giants from 1957 – 1963 and then he was a coach for a number of NFL teams including the Pittsburgh Steelers. We won our last four games to go 7-3 on the year. One of those victories came to Gannon University where I scored one touchdown and rushed for 100 yards. My touchdown run also happened to break Tim Ruth's Career Rushing Record. I was the first Black Running Back to set all of these record at Mercyhurst College and I couldn't do any of it without all of my teammates. Even though that was the pinnacle of my college career, the best moment came in the final game against CW Post. There was a defensive Back that would make a tackle for their team and he would look at our sidelines and flex his muscles. He wore #33. I never caught his name. I had my immature moments show boating and doing touchdown dances and the Heisman Pose and things, but Coach Kimball's teams now played with class and respect. We were taught to keep it within the confines of the game. Well we were down by three with about a minute left in the game and we were driving in CW Post's territory. We still ran the option better than most teams. That was our bread and butter. Our Quarterback, Matt Golga was leading us down the field. We were at the five yard line and Matt called option right. I was just hoping he would pitch me the ball. His read was on the defensive end. He called hike, his eyes went to the defensive end, I kept proper pitch position and I saw the end step towards Matt. He held the ball in order to draw the end in a little more and he pitched it to me. Secure the Ball Wood, I said to myself. I caught the ball and took a few steps and it was me and #33 the defensive back meeting at the goal line. I ran as fast as I could and beat him to the goal line, but I remembered all of the disrespectful things he did to our team. Going full speed I ran right into him and popped him back about four yards in the air. He landed at the back of the end zone and instead of doing a touchdown dance, I just stopped and stared at him, smiled and gave the ball to the referee. I had become a mature young man and Coach Kimball couldn't have been prouder of me. We were told if we won that game we would play the winner of the Bentley vs. Stonehill game. Stonehill ended up upsetting Bentley and the ECAC Commission decided to have Stonehill and Bentley play in the ECAC Bowl game since they split during the regular season. I found this out the next morning in the paper. That meant our season was over.

I was invited to play in a National All-Star Classic that featured Division I and Division II players. There was an NFL Combine out there as well and I took part in that and was noticed by one of the Pittsburgh Steelers Scouts. He contacted our coaching staff and I was invited to a free agent workout with the Steelers along with one of my teammates. Center Chris (Beef) Vlasic. What an experience that was. Coach Cowher was there, we were at Three Rivers Stadium, but ironically that day the Steelers signed Jerome Bettis to their squad. Needless to say, I didn't make the team, but accomplished more than many football college players do every year. Most people don't know how an NFL Combine is conducted. They weighed us, measured our height and put us into groups by our position. They checked our strength by having us bench press 225 lbs. as many times as we could. I finished with 18 repetitions. We then had our vertical leap checked. We raised our hand standing next to a pole that had tabs on it an inch a part. We hit the tab standing with both heels on the ground. We then had to jump straight up in the air, with no steps taken, just straight up in the air and hit the highest tab. Once we hit the highest tab, they measured from the original tab we started at to the highest tab and the distance between the two tabs was out vertical leap. After we left the weight room we went to the field. One of the most amazing sights I saw was walking through the tunnel, underneath the stands, coming out onto the field. It was incredible. I loved the Steelers and loved just being there. When we got on the field, they had us break up into our positional groups. I was with the running backs. It was time to run the 40 yard dash and do the shuttle run. Running the 40 yard dash was extremely intimidating because of how they set it up. They had a coach, on the right and left of us every 5 yards with a stop watch. At the very end, Coach Bill Cowher was standing there with a stopwatch as well. It was like we were running down a tunnel. I ran a 4.45 that day matching my fastest time ever. The shuttle run was designed to check our change of direction ability as well as our start and stop speed. For example, we started at the five yard line, we would sprint to the ten yard line, turn and sprint to the goal line, then turn and sprint back through the five yard line again. The drill covered 20 yards and a good time was crucial for specialty positions. Finally they had the running backs match up with the linebackers. We ran pass routes and did handoff and pitch drills. I was at Three Rivers Stadium and it was amazing.

I had a tryout with the Hamilton Tiger Cats in the CFL as well, but only two players out of the 200 that tried out were signed that day. I was up there with my friend Ric Giles. Football was now over with. I played in some Flag Football leagues with some great players like Jody Dickerson, Otha Davidson, Georj Lewis all from Edinboro as well as Mike Parker Sr., who is an Allegheny Hall of Famer, Bronze Simpson basketball star from Gannon University and local talents Earl Hollis, as well as Tim Cook, and Mike Vaughn from Penn State Behrend. Now it was time to get a job!

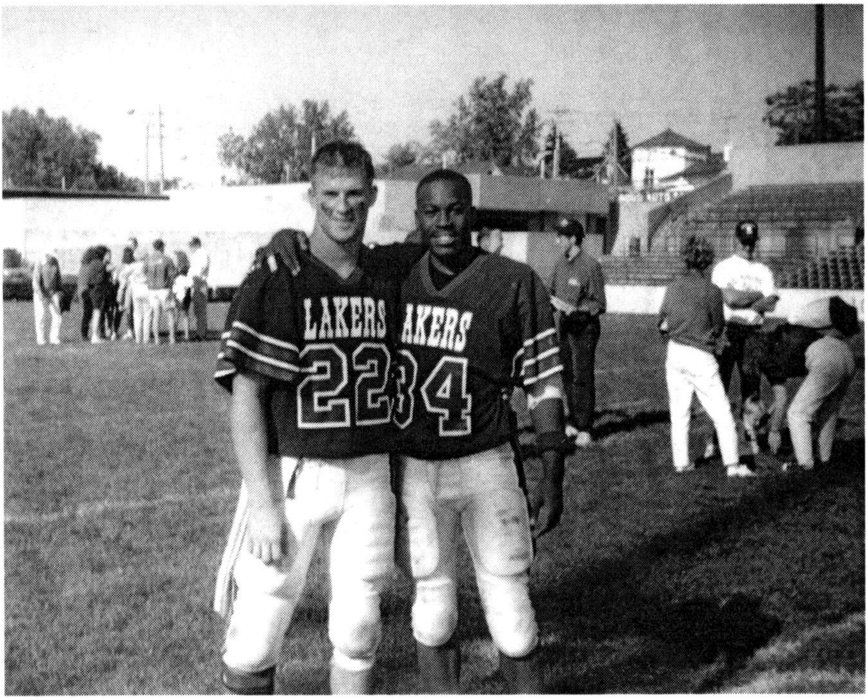
LAKERS
22
AKERS
34

College Years Key Points

- Stay focused on your goals and evaluate where you stand periodically.

- Your independence in College can lead to your success or your demise.

- There will always be something or someone in the way of your dreams, overcome obstacles through hard work and self motivation.

- Prepare yourself for your future through the things that you touch today.

- Carry yourself with a confident swag, which is more appealing than a cocky attitude.

- Be the first one on the field or court for practice and be the last one to leave.

My Career

    IN THE SUMMER OF 1996, I did my internship with then Sports Director Gary Drapcho at WSEE in Erie, Pa. It was a great learning experience. I decided that I wanted to be a Sports Broadcaster. This was something that I knew I could enjoy. I spent a lot of time working at the TV Station. I worked with Lisa Zompa, Scott Bremner, and the Late Great Journalists Freda Tarbell and Carol Pella just to name a few. Gary taught me a lot about what goes on behind the scenes. I did a ton of video shooting at the Seawolves games and got some interviews as well. The one thing I learned about this business was you HAVE to hit your deadlines. The day my internship was done, Gary offered me a job as a part time photographer. He said Woody this will help get your feet in the door. I was only getting paid about $5.50 an hour I believe, but I accepted the position. Every chance I got I would put together my own sports stories, I would sit on the set and read Bill Flanagan's script after he anchored the 6:00 weekend sports. I compiled a bunch of my own stories as I built my resume tape. I made it known that I wanted to be an on-air personality. I thought my prayers had been answered when I heard that Bill was leaving and taking the Cathedral Prep Athletic Director position. I put in for the job and I didn't get it. They said I wasn't ready. I was devastated, but still highly motivated. I would run into Gary Horton from time to time since he was the Mayor's Assistant. He was also my friend Khyl Horton's Uncle. I told him that I wanted to be on-air. He worked at WSEE in the past and knew Freda Tarbell very well. She was now the Assignment Editor over at WICU-TV12. They were looking for a News Reporter. One day I got a call from the News Director Mike Conway. He asked if I had anything on tape that they could look at. I told him that I did a ton of stories on my own and I do have them on tape. I told him that they weren't the best, but with more practice I will fine tune my craft and I will be the best. He then scheduled an interview with me. At this time in 1996, there were zero African American Newscasters in our market. My good friend Mike Ruzzi, who was the Sports Director at WICU, spoke to Mike Conway and said, "We have to bring Craig Woodard on board." I knew that this was a great opportunity for me to give back to my community and continue to open doors for other people of color. I was up for the challenge. One key question I was asked during our interview was, "What do you think about being the only Black On-Air Personality on the news in Erie?" I said to Mike, "I kind of figured you would ask me this question. Whether people are watching me to see how I sound, or they tune in to see what I'm wearing or they watch our station because they know me from growing up in Erie and playing ball or if they are watching to see if I mess up, THE FACT IS THAT THEY ARE WATCHING AND THAT'S WHAT YOU WANT RIGHT?" A big smile came across Mike's face and he said I now see why Mike Ruzzi told me we have to bring you onboard. He said, "The job is yours". I was elated! Thank you Mike Conway for giving me that opportunity and thank you Gary Drapcho and Mike Ruzzi for believing in me.

As a News Reporter I covered City Hall as part of my duties. I did interviews with the Mayor and with the Police Chief. I was learning more about the business each and every day. I also saw how tough your skin had to be after covering some very disturbing stories. I broke some exclusive stories in my final two weeks as a News Reporter before accepting the Fox Sports Anchor job. We were running both NBC and Fox out of the same studio. Mike Ruzzi took part in bringing me on his team. Mike Ruzzi is a true professional and a very dear friend. He took time to share his years of experience with me and shaped who I wanted to become. I was the flashier type of sports guy that liked to use off the wall jargon to catch viewer's attention. I was a big fan of Stuart Scott and thought, wait a minute. There are no Sports Anchors with that type of style on local TV. I wanted to be that for our viewers so I stepped out on a limb and let my personality take over. Ruzz let me do whatever I wanted to do and he never held me back. I started to get a ton of compliments out on the street. Viewers started to notice me and it was kind of nice when people would mention a story that they saw me do. Me being from the Erie Community, I thought back to when I was in 8th Grade at St. Patrick's. I remember turning the news on after we won the City Championship and I wondered why we were not being shown on TV. I had the perfect idea and Ruzz loved it. I asked him if I could start putting highlights of the younger kids on television from Bay City Football, the Parochial League Sports, MYAA and Little League. He said, "Absolutely." I made a few calls and got the schedules and I started featuring the younger kids on the news on a regular basis. I even gave some of these kid's nicknames and they loved it. After my sports shows ran on the weekends, on Monday's we had so many requests from parents who wanted a copy of the show because their son or daughter made the highlights. I tapped into a market that was wide open. I featured players in grade school that the other guys were forced to cover in High School. Athletes like, Bob Sanders, Jovon Johnson, Chelsea Gordon, and Erin Kerner just to name a few. They were local greats and they all played on the national level. This was my way of giving back to my community and everywhere I went I had the support of the Erie community.

During this time I got married and had two boys. Dante' and Jordan Woodard. I was now a father and I could not believe how it felt to be responsible for another life. My kids were everything to me. I was such a proud father. Dante' was born on February 11, 2000. My first born Son. Jordan was born July 23, 2001. They were 17 and a half months apart. Talk about being busy. I used to take my boys everywhere. It seemed like every time I went to the mall people would call them twins. They did favor each other when they were young and Jordan ended up being the same size as Dante' when they were little. Jordan grew so fast. I worked 2nd shift so I was able to take care of them during the day until about 2:00 and when I got home around midnight, if they got up I would put them back to sleep. When both Dante' and Jordan were born, there was one special friend in my life that I wanted to name as their Godfather. His name is Jeff Sansom. Jeff and I knew each other since 6th grade. He went to St. John's while I attended St. Patrick and we played Soccer against each other. Jeff and I would always talk after our games. We respected each other and I was thrilled when I found out he was going to Mercyhurst Prep as well. He became one of my closest friends. He took the role of Dante' and Jordan's Godfather very serious. He would always come over when he could in order to see the kids. He would send the boys cards and gifts on their birthdays and on Christmas and would call to speak with them consistently. Jeff was a good friend, a wonderful Godfather and he was one that I considered my brother.

In 2000 I was given the Distinguished Alumni Award at Mercyhurst Prep. What a true honor to receive this award. I was able to have my Son Dante' in attendance along with my Mom, my Dad travelled up from Kutztown to attend, my Aunt Bettie came along with my Uncle Elmer and my cousin Kevin. This same year my dream of playing professional football came true. I had been out of school for 4 years at that time when I heard that Erie was getting a franchise in the newly formed Indoor Football League. The team was called the Erie Invaders. I went and tried out for the team and I was offered a one year contract. I had to get this cleared by WICU first. I went to Mike Ruzzi, Phil Hayes my new News Director and our General Manager Sandy Benton and asked for their blessing to play. It was a 14 game schedule, 7 home games and 7 away and they said they would work with me in order to make this happen. What incredible people they were to let me live out a dream. Getting paid to play football. We got paid $300 a game and we ended up playing 15 games that year so it was definitely like a part time job. We had to make appearances all over the city, sign autographs after the game and getting to know everyone on the team gave me some insight on what stories I could do when I interviewed them. I was named the Invaders starting Fullback and my main responsibility was to block for our running back Rafael Cooper. At this time I was about 235 lbs. and I was a load to bring down. Coop and I were called Thunder and Lightning. I brought the Thunder with some monster runs and he brought the Lightning since he was so fast and had quick cuts. I ended the season with 9 touchdowns and we lost in the first round of the playoffs. Rafael Cooper went on to play in the NFL with the Green Bay Packers and the Detroit Lions. We still keep in touch today. The Arena Football League ended up buying out the IFL so Erie was without a team for a few years to come. That meant officially my playing days were over. On a positive note, my Mother got a chance to see me play for the first time in her life. We played on Mother's Day weekend that year and I invited her to the game. We ended up playing against Flint, Michigan and I scored two touchdowns. The first time I scored a touchdown I gave the ball to my Mom. She just smiled from ear to ear. She was a proud Mother. After the game she told me if she could do things all over again, she would. That was enough for me to forgive her for not seeing me play until I was an adult. She was now one of my biggest fans. She still has the game ball that I gave her at her apartment.

In August of 2003 I decided to step away from the broadcast industry. I wanted to work more of a regular 9am to 5pm job. I was hired as an Account Executive at Beneficial Finance down in Kittanning, PA. I was only there for 10 months before being promoted to Branch Manager in the Harborcreek, PA office in June of 2004. This is when I bought my first house on East Gore Rd. I didn't know much about the business at the time, but I knew how to communicate with people and I was a good manager. I studied my craft and learned from more experienced employees in the business. In 2006 the highlight of my Athletic career came true. I was a first ballot nominee for the Pennsylvania Erie Metro Chapter Sports Hall of Fame. I could not believe it. My good friend Mike Ruzzi called me to share the great news. I was ecstatic just being nominated, but the best news was the fact that I became a finalist. I was being inducted into the Hall of Fame for my efforts on the basketball court, taking part in track and field and my performance on the football field at Mercyhurst Prep and Mercyhurst College. On that night, I was surrounded by family and friends. I had teammates there to support me, my parents were in attendance and my Grandfather Herman Woodard actually came to see me inducted at the age of 84. I was blessed and living on cloud nine.

Also in 2006, I decided to go back to school and earn my Master's Degree. I was accepted into and accelerated program at American Intercontinental University. It was the longest 10 months of my life. While working full time, I took online classes full time and dedicated myself to my education. I completed my degree in April 2007 earning a 3.87 GPA. I now had a Bachelor Degree in Communication and an MBA in Management. Talk about perfect timing. I applied for a job with American General Finance, who was one of our competitors, in Fayetteville, NC. I got the job and had to relocate to North Carolina in

May 2007 where I bought my 2nd house. After working there for two years as a Branch Manager, I was promoted to District Manager and I was in charge of ten offices. After a few months in my new position I began to notice that my marriage was on the rocks. This is where my life took a major change and it all happened for a good reason.

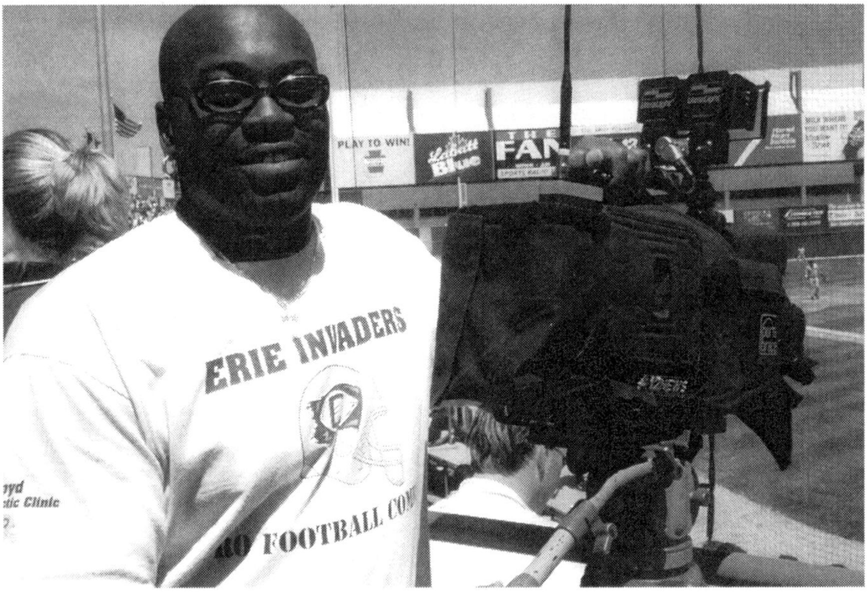
ERIE INVADERS
PLAY TO WIN!
Labatt Blue

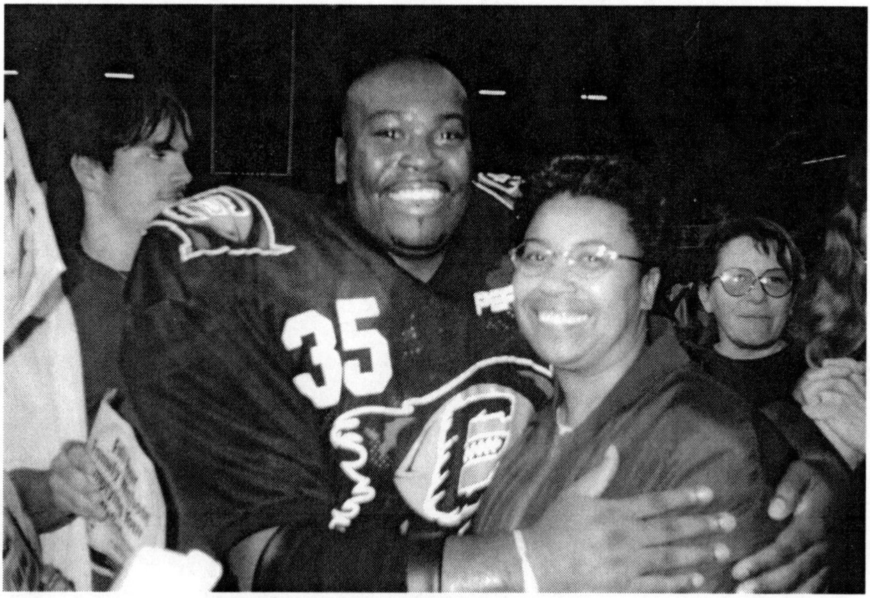
35

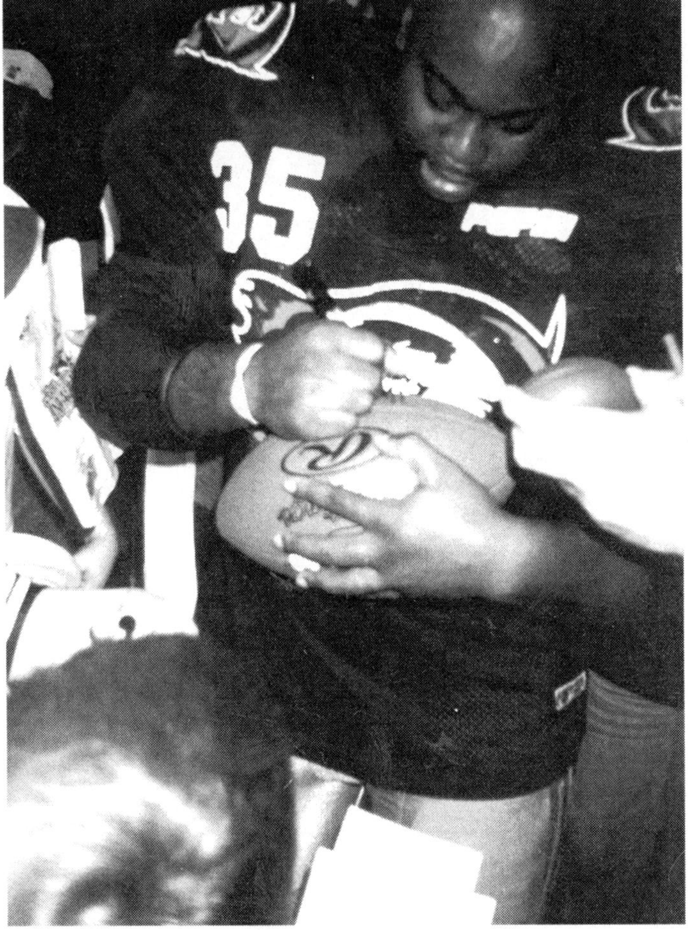
35

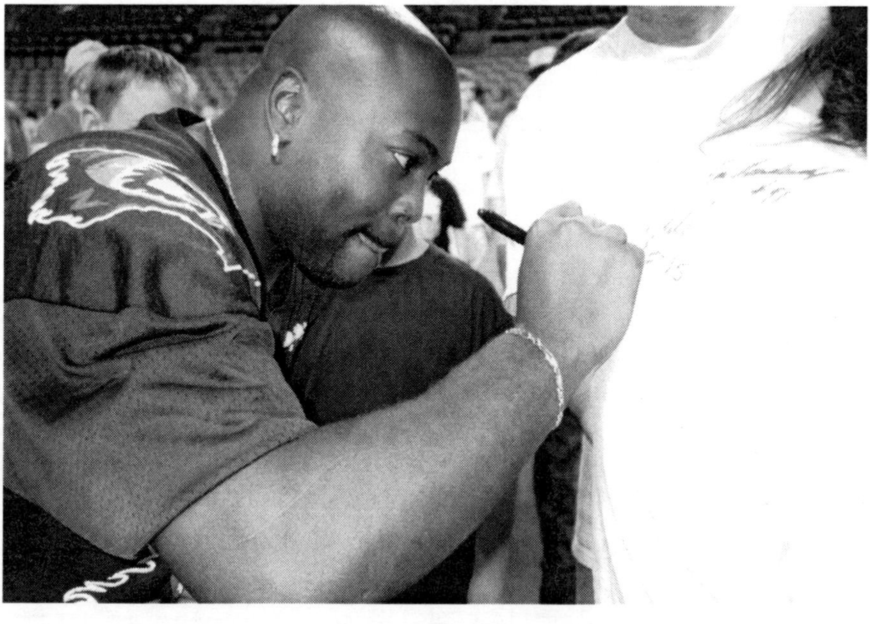

My Career Key Points

- Always put your family first.

- Work hard every day knowing that your family is your motivation.

- Follow your dreams and never let anyone tell you that you can't do something.

- With success comes great sacrifice. Be prepared to give something up in order to achieve it all.

- Be conscious of where your children are in life so you can minimize change which secures stability for them.

- Putting your dreams on hold in order for your kids to have a stable life doesn't mean that you stop dreaming. When they grow older and go off to College, make sure you pick up your dream where you left off.

- Failing to plan is planning to fail.

- Set achievable goals, reach them then don't settle. Now it's time to set higher goals.

The Divorce

SOME DIVORCES END UP being civil and some end up being devastating. Mine ended up being a nightmare, not just because I had children involved, but because the boys and I experienced something that I wish no parent would ever have to experience. I'm going to let you into my world for a little bit, but in order to do so I am going to change the names of a few characters throughout this chapter. When you finish the next two chapters you will know why I chose to do this. Sit back, relax and be prepared to read the next few chapters at one sitting. This life experience will keep you on the edge of your seat and take you through a range of emotions during this journey. Where do I begin?

When I stated in the last chapter that I noticed my marriage was on the rocks, what I meant by that is my wife Mary and I were separated before and headed towards that once again. Around Thanksgiving time in 2009 we sat down and had a discussion about being unhappy. Now here is my 8-Mile moment. I call it my 8-Mile moment because I get to talk about all of the bad things and character flaws that I have and that gives no one else anything bad to say about me since I've said it already. Just like Eminem in the movie 8-Mile. I'm a very strong minded individual and I'm very stubborn. I have put in work on this to improve over the years, but I like things a certain way and I question absolutely everything. I never like for anyone to raise their voice with me and I hate to argue about little things. I would rather dismiss the little things because life is way too short to worry about them. Other than my misfortunate situation concerning my stepmother back when I was in 3rd grade, I have never put my hands on a woman in an abusive way in my life. That is me in a nut shell. My dirty laundry is on the floor. I own how I am and trust me, I try to improve myself daily. The first step of improving yourself is to recognize that you need to improve and I have done that.

So back to our conversation about not being happy. Mary and I both agreed that it would be best to go our separate ways. I owned the house, since it was in my name, and she couldn't afford to live there by herself so she chose to move out. There was something in the back of my mind that kept asking why was she moving so quickly? I paid it no attention because I knew that this was best and I was unhappy for years as well and I was just going through the motions. My concern was how well these kids would cope with the change. I didn't want them to feel like my Sister Angie and I felt when our parents got divorced. I didn't want them to blame themselves when this had nothing to do with them. Any time I thought about being away from my children I would cry. How would I be able to maintain and be strong for them? It was very tough knowing that I wouldn't have them in the house every single day, but I did all I could to reassure them that everything would be alright. She wanted to take a few months to get her move together and finally in the middle of January 2010 she moved out and got her own place. At this point, we were trying to be as civil as possible for the boys. I even helped move some of the boy's things out of the house. They kept their bedroom sets and everything at my house since my house was all they knew. That was their comfort zone and their stability.

I was now a single father, just like my Dad was when he had me. The kids stayed with her on Monday and Tuesday and they were with me on Wednesday and Thursday and we alternated weekends. When she moved out I continued to pay her car payment which was $626 a month since the vehicle was in my name. We agreed that there would be no child support paid by either of us since we had the boy's equal time. I took care of the boys financially when they were with me and she took care of the boys financially when they were with her. She moved out on a Saturday, the following week her Mother came to visit her and on Friday she both went to pick the boys up from school since it was her weekend. I was told, by one of my neighbors whom was mutual friends of ours, that she introduced her Mom to her new boyfriend. He told me that she was bragging to him saying that her Mom really liked him and that he looked at her like she was the only woman alive. Let me rewind, so she introduced her Mom to her new boyfriend less than a week after she moved out of my house. To me, it was clear that something was going on and my neighbor confirmed it when he told me she cheated on me. At this point my only concern was my children. Months went by and she became open about who she was dating. I went out on a few dinner dates myself, but I wanted to be very particular about my kids. I wanted the next woman that I chose to bring into my children's lives to be someone that was truly special. Our divorce was finalized in July 2010 and Mary lied on the court documents in order to move the divorce right along. In the state of North Carolina you had to be legally separated for at least 12 months. She lied to the Judge under oath in order to get out of the marriage sooner. Two nights before my divorce hearing was scheduled for I was checking out Facebook. I got a notification from my college sweetheart talking about how good Moscato Wine is and that her Mom introduced that to her. I hadn't spoken to her in years. Her name is Christine Gile. I pulled up her page and looked through her pictures and she looked absolutely beautiful. We dated for close to a year my junior year at the Hurst. She went to Indiana University in Indiana, PA so we were about two and a half hours away. We ended up breaking up and going our separate ways back in college. I always loved Christine and had a great time with her. She was the one female that kept it real 100% of the time and I couldn't stop myself from thinking about what I missed out on by us breaking up. She sent me an inbox message on Facebook and I responded and we caught back up sending messages to each other for a few hours. It was like old times once again. She lost her cat a few days prior to this and I was helping her through that tough time. I told her if she ever wanted to talk she could call me any time and I gave her my number. She responded, "I'm going to call right now!" A huge smile came on my face. In less than a minute my phone rang and I heard her voice for the first time since 1995. Fifteen years went by and I was on the phone with my college love. We spoke on the phone all night that night. We got off the phone in the morning and got some sleep then got back on the phone and spoke with one another all day. She was living in Tampa, FL at the time so we were ten hours away. We caught up with each other and I told her about my divorce coming up and she supported me in everything that I did. I knew that I had reconnected with my soul mate, my ride or die chick, the one that would be with me and have my back through anything. The following day I went to court, the divorce hearing lasted for only about 20 minutes, the document was signed by the judge and recorded downstairs at the clerk's office. This is when it all began.

The Divorce Key Points

- People change and that's okay. It's not the end of the world.

- Parents realize that children are affected when their parents get a divorce.

- Family counseling always has its benefits. Don't be too proud to take part. If you don't go for yourself, go for your children.

- Make sure your kids are kept as the top priority.

- There is someone out there for everyone. Just be patient.

- Never stay in a relationship strictly for the kid's sake. They can see through it all and ultimately want each parent to be happy.

Fighting for Custody

THIS CHAPTER IS BASED on documented facts, life experiences and real situations. This was a tough chapter for me to write, but rest assured it was therapeutic as well as much needed. I had to share this climactic point in our lives in order to let you all know how good God has been to me. He put a woman back into my life on purpose. I could not have gotten through this chapter of my life without my best friend Chrissy. She was and still is my main support system and was always there for me as a sounding board as we strategically planned out our next move. In my soul, I have already forgiven Darcy for the pain and turmoil that she put the kids, Chrissy and me through. That forgiveness is for me to move on. However, as a man and the father of these wonderful kids, I will never forget what has been done. This is our story!

My divorce was final in July 2010 and I was already planning a trip to Florida for the first time in my life. I was going to go reconnect with my College Sweetheart Christine Gile. She and I spoke on the phone very often. We kept in touch and worked on our long distance courtship. Christine called me on the phone one night and asked when I could come to Tampa. I told her the dates I was planning on coming and while we were talking on the phone she was booking my flight. She sent me a confirmation email and told me to check my email. I looked at it and immediately got butterflies. I laughed so hard. What a surprise. The second week of August 2010 I was going to Tampa. I couldn't wait. Until then we continued to talk on the phone and I told her about my kids and how special they were to me. I used to sing to her on the phone and she would sing right back. We reminisced like we were in college again. All of my original feelings for her had come back. It was such an incredible feeling. The day had finally come, I was flying to Tampa out of Raleigh, NC. I was nervous as ever, but truly excited to see Chrissy. I arrived at the Tampa airport and walked down to baggage claim. She told me she would meet me there. Remember, it had been 15 years or so since I saw her last. I got off of the escalator and looked over by the seats and there she was staring right at me. I smiled from ear to ear. She came walking over and I gave her a huge hug and kiss. Damn she smelled so good and looked outstanding. How did the Lord bless me a 2nd time? To have this opportunity later in life after I grew up a bit and experienced a lot in my life was a blessing from God. I was not going to mess this opportunity up like I did in college.

We had the entire long weekend together, we had beautiful Florida weather and most important, we had each other. What a great time we had in Tampa. We went everywhere. On our first night we ended up on St. Pete Beach. We drank Moscato and took pictures while listening to some old school music which we both love. It was perfect. The bad thing about visiting somewhere or going on vacation is that the time does fly when you are having fun. Before I knew it, it was Monday and time to fly back home. I have to be honest with you. I had a real tough time saying goodbye to Chrissy. We had so much fun. I knew after my experience with her in Florida that this is somewhere I could live and get used to life with her by my side. I flew back home and continued to stay in touch with her. We already started planning my next visit which was in about 3 weeks. It felt like the longest three weeks ever. I told my kids that I got back together with my college sweetheart and they couldn't wait to meet her. I had known Chrissy for 16 years at the time and I'm the type of person that follows my heart while trusting my gut. She was the ONE! She was the one that got away in college and the one that I got a 2nd chance with. She was the one that I needed in my life and the one that I knew I could grow old with. She was the one that would always have my back no matter what and the one to lift me up when I was down. We shared everything together. We became best friends in such a short period of time. The chemistry that we shared with one another was insane. I knew that I had to make her mine. She was the one that I would marry. I had already started to build my relationship with her Mother Karen Erdley. We spoke on the phone a number of times and she was such a great woman. One Sunday when Dante' was over at the house with me I asked him what he thought about me getting married again. Keep in mind, he had never met Chrissy, nor had his brother Jordan. Dante's reply to me was that he thought it was a great idea because he wanted me to be happy. I gave him a big hug and I said, "Come on let's go buy Chrissy a ring. You can help me pick it out." He was so excited. We went ring shopping and after looking at many of them at several different stores, I came across one that jumped out at me. I showed it to Dante', who was 10 years old at the time, and he said, "That's the one Dad." He was right. I fell in love with this ring and I could just imagine how it would look on her finger. After I bought it, I kept opening the box and looking at it. It was beautiful just like Chrissy. I was wondering what she would say. See Chrissy was never married and didn't have any children. She was a school teacher in Tampa and just earned her Master Degree in Educational Leadership. I found out how much she really loved me back in the day when I came to visit her. She told me how upset she was with me for leaving the relationship and moving on especially for marrying Mary Cook. They were from the same hometown and they didn't care for each other.

Now that I had the ring there were two more things I had to do. As an old school gentleman, I wanted to do this the right way and show the respect that I had for her Mom. Christine didn't communicate with her father anymore so I called her Mom up and I asked her for her blessing to ask Chrissy to marry me. Karen told me, "Craig you are a good man and my daughter has always loved you. I support you in this, but Chrissy is a grown woman and you know my daughter. She is going to make this decision on her own." We laughed a little bit and continued to talk and I told her that I was going to ask her to marry me on my next trip to Tampa which was on September 10, 2010. I flew out of Raleigh, NC on September 9, 2010 and I arrived in Tampa later on that night. It was so good to see her. I had to do some scrambling now, how can I make this as romantic as possible and give her the proposal she has been waiting for all of her life? Well Friday morning came and I kept running ideas through my head. Finally it hit me. I called the Melting Pot and set up reservations for two for that night at 7:00. I told her that I wanted to take her to dinner that night and let her know that I wanted to go to the Melting Pot since I love that place. We were running a little bit late as usual so I called the restaurant to let them know. When we arrived, I had the ring in the box and it was in my pocket. It was almost show time. We walked in and they sat us in a very private section of the restaurant. The mood was perfect. I had flowers waiting for her at the table, we sat down and right as we got settled she looked at me and said, "I have to go to the bathroom." I laughed my butt off, so I got out of the booth and let her out and I knew I was going to propose when she came back. I pulled out the box and I set it on the seat right next to where she was sitting. She came back to the table and I let her in and she slid right over to her seat. I said to her, "You saw it huh?" She said, "Saw what?" I reached over and grabbed the box from under the table and said, "Saw this!" I opened the box and there was bling bling for days. A beautiful diamond ring. I told her, while fighting back the tears as best as I could, that I loved her with all my heart. She stole my heart again and I will never let you go like I did before. I said that I knew we had only been dating for a very short time, but I know what I want and what I want is for you to be my Wife forever. I then said those four words that I had been so excited to say! I asked, "Will you marry me?" She started crying and said YES! We hugged and kissed and hugged some more and right at that moment our waiter came to our table. He saw what was going on and I told him she said yes so he took our picture for us. What a great time that was. Very special. I called the kids and told them the great news and let them know that she said yes.

Of course they told their Mom Mary what was going on and on Monday when I returned to Fayetteville, I was served with child support papers. The day I returned you guys. Like they say on NFL Countdown. "Come on Man!" She now had started asking me to pay her money for the kids when she had the kids the same exact time as me. I had only seven payments left on her car and she would have owned it free and clear. She took the Grand Caravan and traded it in for a Brand New Ford Fusion and she wanted me to pay her the exact amount her new car payment was. I wasn't having it. I kept records of everything I did and everything I bought the boys. I also kept a calendar of the overnight stays the boys had at my house. I knew this would come in handy when I got to court. She had been talking with her friends and family and someone convinced her to take me to court. By the way, every single day that the kids spent the night at her apartment, I would drive over to see them after I got out of work just to say goodnight in person. I couldn't stand not being able to see them when I lived in the same city. That's the type of father I am. Darcy was also upset that I had to have her removed from my benefits at work since the divorce was final. She was upset with me since she had to pay for her own insurance. She told the kids that I can only see them on the porch when I would come over since she was no longer on my benefits.

As time went on, I was told that Mary was dating a guy. His name is Wendell Jones. As a Dad, I took it upon myself to try to reach out and meet this guy since he was a part of my children's life. My first attempt to meet him failed after I told Dante' to go inside and tell him that I would like to meet him. Mary told him to tell me that Wendell was sleeping. Dante' came and told him and also admitted that he wasn't sleeping. I didn't make a big deal about it, I just got the boys and left the parking lot. The next time I was supposed to meet him was on the following Sunday when Mary came to pick the kids up. He was supposed to come with her, but he never showed up. On Wednesday, when I went to pick the kids up, Dante' and Jordan came to the door. I asked them if Wendell was home and they said yes. I told Dante' to tell Wendell that I would like to meet him. After a few minutes Wendell came to the door and I shook his hand and said, "What's up Wendell, I'm Craig it's nice to meet you!" We began talking and I asked him a few questions and let him know that I didn't want him to put his hands on my kids. I told him that if there is an issue with the boys that needs handled just call me. We exchanged phone numbers and I had the boys come out of the car to where we were standing. I told them that they need to respect Wendell just like they do me. I told them that I didn't want them to talk back to him or their Mom and I asked them if they understood me. They both said, "Yes." I told them to get back in the car. I wrapped up my conversation with Wendell, but I recalled that during the conversation he kept telling me that he played football at East Carolina University. He said it about four times. I didn't catch on until we were driving home. I kept wondering why he kept saying that to me. I thought that maybe my kids were bragging about me playing College and Pro Football so he felt the need to tell me about what he did on the grid iron. I couldn't put my finger on it.

On October 18, 2010, I called Chrissy after I cooked dinner for the kids and after I got them settled for bed. I told her about my conversation with Wendell. Now keep in mind, I have to give Chrissy so much credit for helping me through this difficult situation. This is why I married this woman. She was my best friend. I recapped the conversation with her and told her that he kept telling me about him playing at ECU. I told her to try to pull up the ECU roster from 1990 – 1999. His name was nowhere on the roster. That was a red flag for me. We got off the phone and I told her I would call her later on. Chrissy took the information that I told her and she began to question the validity of his statements. She began digging and doing more extensive research. Around 10:30 that evening Chrissy called me back up. We started talking for a little bit and she asked me how close I was to Milton Dr. I told her I was only a few miles from there. She told me to get into my car and drive over there and tell her what I saw. So I drive over there and I come up to a White house on the corner. There was an old beat up car in the yard and the front light was on. I described what I saw to her and she asked me if I would remember what he looked like if I saw him again? I told her that I would. She said, "Hang up your phone, I'm going to send you an email and when you get the picture call me right back." So I hung up the phone and my email notification went off. I opened up my email and there was a picture of Wendell Jones. I was like, "Damnnnnnn she's good!" I called her back and said, "Wow honey you are good, where did you find that picture?" Okay folks, this is where my life changed forever!

Chrissy said to me, "Honey I don't know how to tell you this, but I looked his name up on the North Carolina Sex Offender Website and his picture and information all came up." I have to tell you all, my heart dropped and skipped a few beats for about a minute straight. I immediately started to get hot as I started sweating. I was silent for a little bit and Chrissy kept saying, Honey are you okay?" I finally answered her and I felt a rage that I never felt in my entire life. The reason why I felt this way is because my children were over there with him. Wendell Jones was a Registered Sex Offender that had just been released from prison about a year prior and he was sleeping in the same apartment as my kids. What do I do? There were so many thoughts that ran through my mind at this point. I couldn't believe that my kids were in this situation. I told Chrissy I would call her back while I figured out my next move. I drove home and thought long and hard about how I would handle this situation. I googled his name and there he was. A registered sex offender. This is the guy that Mary chose to be with. This is why she rushed the divorce. It all made sense to me now. The first thing I could think of was to go next door to my neighbor's house. He and his Wife were mutual friends of ours. It was about 11:30 at night now and all of the lights were out at their house, but I knocked on the door anyway since this was an emergency. I knocked and knocked and no one came to the door. I then ran across the street to my other neighbor's home. They were mutual friends of ours as well.

When I knocked on the door, Charlie came to the door and I said to him, "Yo, Man you are never going to believe this, come here." He walked across the street with me and I showed him my computer screen. He said, "Who is that?" I said, "That is Mary's new boyfriend and I think he is with my kids right now!" He said, "Hold up, let me go get Tamara so she could see this." Tamara was his wife and Mary's good friend. Tamara came over to the house as well and she saw all of the information. She was stunned! We walked outside and we were standing in the driveway when Tamara said, "Does Mary know that he is a registered Sex Offender?" I said, "I don't know." She then said that if she didn't know herself, she would want to know. She said, "Let me call her." So Tamara grabbed Charlie's cell phone and dialed Mary's number. It went to voicemail so she left a message for her to call her back. In less than a minute Mary called back and Tamara answered the phone. It was on speaker phone so I heard the conversation word for word and this is how the conversation went.

Tamara: Hello?

Mary: Hey what's going on?

Tamara: Is Wendell there with you?

Mary: Yeah why?

Tamara: I need you to go into the living room for a minute.

Mary: Okay, hold on. (Walks into the living room).

Mary: Okay, what's up?

Tamara: I found out tonight that Wendell is a registered sex offender.

Mary: Oh yeah. I know. What happened was, he and about five or six of his friends were at a bachelor party a few years ago and there was a stripper there. The stripper started dancing and one of the guys exposed himself to the stripper. She ended up being 16 years old. When she left, she told her Aunt what happened and her Aunt brought her back to the party to identify the guy that exposed himself. She couldn't remember which one did it. So her Aunt called the cops and they all got arrested and charged and they went to prison and had to register as sex offenders, but he is in the process of getting the charges expunged.

Tamara: Wait a minute, so you knew?

Mary: Yes I knew, but he said he didn't do anything.

Tamara: Okay, well the problem is not the fact that I found out. The problem is that Craig found out.

Mary: How the hell did he find out?

Tamara: Darcy, anyone can find out. They have this information all on the internet.

Mary: Let me call you back.

At this point folks, I was going out of my mind. All I could think of was how I could get my kids out of this house? I called the Sheriff Department and spoke to a deputy and explained to him what I found out and that I wanted to get my kids out of the house. While on the phone with him, Mary called Tamara back. She woke up Wendell and had him leave the house. I asked the Sheriff what my options were. He told me that since the sex offender unit was not going to be in until the morning the only thing I could do was call her and ask her if I could come get the kids for the night. He said that they could come with me so that there is no physical issues, but that they could not help out or interfere. She had to be willing to let the kids come with me. They would also have to see in the morning if he was in violation of his probation. So I got off the phone with the Sheriff and got on Charlie's phone to speak with Mary and ask her if I could come and get the kids. She told me, "Absolutely not!" There was nothing I could do. I didn't sleep at all that night. My mind started wondering and I started thinking whether or not Wendell touched my kids. I also questioned why he never told me about this situation earlier in the day when I was asking him about his past. I felt betrayed and I felt that I let my children down, but the fact was that I couldn't do anything about it at the time. I called Chrissy and she was there for me. She calmed me down and prevented me from doing what every father desires to do in that moment. I wanted to put my hands on this guy. That is a father's normal reaction. I kept asking the Lord to give me strength and guide me through this. I asked the Lord to keep me calm. Chrissy and I spoke on the phone all night that night. She was my rock and my sanity. I never would have been able to go through this experience without her by my side.

In the morning I drove to the boy's school and I told the Principal what was going on. He only seemed concerned with the rest of the students at school saying that Wendell is not allowed on school property or near the campus. I told him that I understood that, but what about my situation with my kids? He had no answers for me. I left the school and I called Children's Services. I told them about the situation and the response I got was mind blowing. The case worker asked me if there were any allegations from my children. I said well no, I haven't had a chance to speak with them yet. I also said sometimes kids don't tell their parents if something happened to them because they are scared to tell. Doesn't that occur all of the time? She said, "Yes you are correct Sir, however I can't help you. Without no allegations, there is no investigation, I'm sorry." Just like that she got off the phone. Unbelievable! The system was failing me folks. What was I going to do? I got to work that day and I couldn't concentrate on anything except for making sure my kids were okay. Chrissy called me on the phone and she said, "I bet she kept them out of school today." I said, "Let me call you back in a few. I will call and check." I called the school and asked if Dante' and Jordan were at school today. One of the ladies in the front office said, "Mr. Woodard due to privacy rules I can't give out that information on the phone." I said, "You can't tell me whether my kids are in school or not?" She said, "No Sir I apologize, but I can have one of their teacher's give you a call." I said, "Great thank you." Within about ten minutes Jordan's teacher called me. She told me that Jordan was not in school today and she checked with Dante's teacher and he didn't make it to school either. I said thank you and hung up. I told me boss I had to leave for an emergency. I drove down to the courthouse and made a phone call to a gentleman in the family court system who helped me fill out the Custody paperwork correctly. I made the decision to file for custody. I had to trust in the court system, this in my mind was doing the right thing. I had a good support system as well. My parents, Chrissy and my best friend Otha Davidson all helped me through this. I was sitting in this gentleman's office and we were talking and something told me to leave. This was my day to get the kids and I usually would pick them up at Mary's apartment. I went downstairs to the clerk's office and filed my paperwork then I ran to the car. This is the weird thing about my trip to her apartment. She lived about ten miles from the courthouse and there were a ton of traffic lights on the way. As I was driving I noticed that I kept hitting Green lights. It was so weird. I got there very quickly and just as I pulled into the parking lot, Mary was pulling out of her parking space with the boys in the car.

    I pulled up next to her and I said, "Where are you going?" She told me that the boys were going to stay with her and she was driving to the airport in Raleigh, NC to pick her Mom up. I was about to lose my mind. Without thinking I put my car in reverse and blocked her car in. I got out of the car with a look on my face that the boys never saw in their lives. I told them to get out of the car and to get into mine. She started screaming and yelling and she made a scene, but the boys did exactly what I said. Let's recap for a minute. So I find out that her boyfriend is a registered sex offender, she knew he was a registered sex offender and the person she chooses to try and keep from the boys is me? Yeah, I didn't understand that concept either. It just didn't make sense. I got the kids in car and got them settled and we all just looked at each other and we started crying. I tried to stay strong for my kids, but I just couldn't take seeing them like this. It was so emotional. We drove home and I sat them down to speak about what happened and I wanted to ask them what they knew about the situation. Immediately the boys started telling me that they were woke up around 6:00 in the morning and their Mom started telling them that I was going to try and take them from her forever. They told me that she explained to them why Wendell wasn't there. They then told me the exact same story about this so called bachelor party that she told Tamara. I was livid. I couldn't believe that she exposed our kids to this nonsense. At that time I let them know the truth, since they had already been exposed to lies and explicit material. Chrissy and I found out, after doing research, court documents stated that Wendell was charged with indecent liberties with children/assault on a female back on January 4, 1997. The girl was only 15 years old. Because she chose not to testify, he was able to plea to a lesser charge. Only a few years later, on April 15, 2004, court transcripts proved he pled guilty to having sex with another 15 year old girl. This child was his girlfriend's God Daughter who was spending the night over at his girlfriend's home. Wendell went into the living room while his girlfriend was asleep at around 1:00 in the morning court documents say. He had sex with her right on the couch. Statutory rape folks. A couple of days went by and the girl told her Grandmother on April 18, 2004 what happened and Wendell was arrested and charged and went to prison for just under two years. He also was now considered a sexual predator and had to register as a sex offender. There are sex offender rules that I was not privy to at the time. I found out the rules later on in this chapter. All of this information was public record and Mary could have done the research on her man like Chrissy and I did in order to get to the truth. I told the kids that I filed for custody and explained what would happen. Dante', who was 10 years old at the time, told me he really didn't like Wendell anyway and he knew there was a reason why. Dante' also told me that Mary left him alone for over an hour with Wendell in the house while she took Jordan to Taekwondo practice. I struggled with hearing these facts folks. My mind went 100 different directions. I then had to ask the tough question. I asked both of the boys if Wendell touched them in any way, physically or sexually and they both said, "NO." I then said, "Are you sure?" They said, yes Dad, we would tell you if something happened." I broke down and cried with them. We hugged and I told them that they don't deserve to be in this situation and that I would always be here for them. They stayed with me for two days and in the process I was served with custody papers. On the paperwork, I noticed that I was actually listed as the Plaintiff. The reason why I was listed as the Plaintiff is because I filed my paperwork before her attorney. The court hearing was set for less than two weeks.

This was the longest two weeks of my life. I checked around and did some research on attorneys in the local area and it is very expensive hiring an attorney for family court. At this time in my life, I had the house to take care of, a car payment and I was left with many of the bills and I felt helpless. I couldn't afford to pay for an attorney. My time was running out. Mary had already called many of her friends and family and she borrowed money by stating to them that I was trying to take the kids from her. That was the furthest from the truth, but her folks would believe anything she said. She even tried to manipulate many of my family and friends through lies and deception. None of my friends bought into it, but there were a few of my family members who couldn't see through her smoke. There are some to this day that have chosen to believe her side of things and we have no communication whatsoever. I really would have hated to see how they would have treated me if I actually did something wrong or if the shoe was on the other foot.

The night before my temporary custody hearing I was speaking with Chrissy on the phone. She and I were doing a ton of research on how to represent yourself in court. It's called "Pro Se." That is a Latin phrase meaning "for oneself." I was now going to represent myself in court against a seasoned attorney in order to get this guy Wendell away from my kids. The point initially was never to gain full custody of my children, it was to protect them from someone she chooses to bring around them. About 1:00 in the morning, Chrissy said to me, "How will you know if you will be able to handle representing yourself in court?" I said, it's simple. First of all, no one knows the facts about this case better than I do. However, I was emotionally attached to this case and that does concern me, but I knew me and I knew what needed to be done. If I wake up in the morning and I have my game face on, I will be fine. If I wake up and think about what I need to do and I breakdown emotionally, then I will go to court and I will ask for a continuance." After we got off of the phone I did research on custody hearings all night long. I reviewed case law, terms, background information and I arranged all of my evidence. I didn't sleep one wink that night. I got in the shower and cleared my mind and yes, I had my game face on. I was ready to go. I drove down to the courthouse and I waited patiently outside the courtroom. The crowd began to grow outside of the courtroom. When they opened the doors, everyone in the hall went inside. That's when I found out that this was considered open court. That's when you sit in the courtroom and wait until your case is called. While you are sitting there you are listening to everyone else's court hearings. It was very intimidating. Finally the time came, my name was called and I went up in front of the Judge. Mary's attorney started things off. She stated to the Judge "That if I wanted to ask for a continuance I needed to do so at that time." I was ready to go. I said, "Your honor I'm ready to proceed." The attorney took the floor and began to acknowledge the fact that Mary made a mistake. She stated that Mary had no idea that Wendell Jones was a registered sex offender and that once she found out they broke up and she no longer has him around the kids. She said she didn't think that Mary should lose custody of the kids for making a mistake. She is kind hearted and took what story Mr. Jones told her and she failed to do her research on his background to validate whether he was telling the truth or not. The Judge then turned to me and asked what my response was. I told her that what she is saying is totally untrue. I heard her say that she knew he was a registered sex offender. I even have the proof of what he did. She has made a poor decision that could have affected the kids and I do not want this guy around my kids again your honor. She asked me if I had any proof to validate my statements. I said absolutely, I gave her attorney a copy and presented a copy to the court. The Judge let me talk about all of the evidence that I had, but prior to that the attorney said, "Your honor I haven't had time to see this evidence." The Judge said, "Take a few minutes and review it. Mr. Woodard please continue." So I did and I proceeded to share with her all of the information I retrieved. It was now time for the Judge to make her decision. She said that she would keep the shared custody in place so that she didn't make any major change to the boy's schedule. But my victory came when she added a provision in the order that stated, "Wendell Jones will no longer be allowed around the kids." I couldn't believe it. I did it. I won. I have now protected my kids from this sexual predator. Court concluded and I walked out into the hallway and Mary started yelling at me. Can you believe that she was upset with the verdict? Most normal Mother's want to keep their children away from sex offenders. Well not in this case! We now had to go to mandatory mediation. That was scheduled for two weeks and the final custody hearing wasn't for another 6-8 months. Custody proceedings can be a long process.

At mediation, I became aware that something didn't seem right. I walked into mediation and met with Mary and the mediator and the mediator asked who wanted to go first and talk about what they wanted out of this session. Scheduling, visitation, custody, etc. Mary said, "He can go first." So I said the one thing that I got in temporary custody and the main thing that surrounded the custody hearing. I said, "I don't want Wendell Jones round my kids." The mediator looked at her and asked if she would agree to that. Darcy said, "No I don't." That's when I got up and said, "I will see you in court." I left because at that point if she still wanted this guy around the kids, there was nothing else I needed to talk about. Incredible. So now the temporary order stays in place until the final hearing. Well about one week later, Dante' and Jordan both started to show bad behavior in school. These boys never got in trouble in school before and now I started getting phone calls from their teachers, they were talking back in class and being aggressive. I would talk to the kids about it and they would tell me all of the prison stories that Wendell told them about things he used to do when he was locked up. He used to cuss at them and would talk to them about beating me up. I had the suspicion that Mary was still sneaking Wendell into her house so one night when Chrissy was watching the kids, I got into my car and drove past her house. I saw Wendell's car in her driveway. I took a picture with my cell phone of his car, his license plate and I positioned the camera view so that you could see her address from her mailbox and his car in the background. I kept that proof just in case I needed it. Now I knew she was still involved with this guy. The kids would never tell me if they saw him or not while over at her house. But a father knows. I could tell when my kids were acting different. Months went by and the kids continued to get in trouble in school. I had a number of meetings with the principal and their teachers. I couldn't continue to put my kids through this any longer. This long custody proceeding was weighing so heavy on everyone. I reached out to Mary and wanted to go back to mediation and end this fiasco for the kid's sake. She agreed to go back to mediation. Before I went to mediation, the boys came over one day and Dante' said to me, "Dad, Wendell and Mom broke up for good this time. They had a big fight and she threw all of his stuff out. They are done now." I said, "Wait a minute. They were still dating?" Dante' told me, "Yes", but they are not together anymore. So going into mediation I was under the impression that Wendell was no longer in the picture. We sat down at mediation and came up with a decent schedule for the boys. For their protection I added a provision that stated before a 3rd party significant other is introduced to or brought around the kids, a thorough background check will be done and provided to the other parent. I added this so that this situation didn't happen again in the future. She agreed. We signed the parenting agreement, had it recorded and all was resolved right? WRONG!

Only days after the parenting agreement was signed I found out that she had moved Wendell into her house months ago. She went against the temporary custody order. I knew my gut feeling was right. However, at this point I couldn't do anything about it because Wendell was no longer a provision in the order. I didn't write his name in there specifically because he was out of the picture, so I thought. She now took advantage of this and had no qualms about it. This next portion of the custody chapter is going to blow your minds. When pushed to the brink of insanity, I still kept my composure and if I did it, you can as well.

Here we go! July 4th weekend 2010 Chrissy and I went to Erie and Kittanning, PA to visit family and friends. The boys stayed with Mary since it was her five day visitation time. When we got back to Fayetteville the boys came over to start our visitation time. The first thing they said when they were dropped off was, "Dad and Chrissy you won't believe what happened." They began to tell us that Wendell twisted Jordan's arm behind his back trying to show him what he did to a guy in prison. He started yelling at him and swearing and he twisted Jordan's arm so far back that Jordan began to cry and tell him to stop. Dante' said he looked at his Mom to do something and she just sat there. Wendell kept twisting his arm until Jordan was on the ground crying and screaming then he finally go. Jordan told me this story and he was crying while telling me this. I was furious. My job is to protect my kids. This sexual predator put his hands on my Son and I didn't think I could contain myself. I picked up the phone and I called Darcy. She tried to down play what happened. I was going off. I was so upset. I then called Children Services and the case worker told me I needed to call the police because that was assault. So I called the Sheriff's Department and we all met with a deputy the next day. The kids told him exactly what he did. I also showed him all of the paper work that Chrissy and I came up with. He sent us down to the Magistrate's office so that we can file charges on Wendell Smith. When we were called to go speak with the Magistrate, she asked to speak with the boys first. After speaking with them she called for me. I went back there and she said that she was going to issue a warrant for his arrest for assault on a child under the age of 12. She asked me what his address was. Not knowing how crucial my answer was going to be, I responded, "Do you want his registered address or the address where he is living at?" The Magistrate said, "Excuse me?" I then repeated, "Do you want his registered address or the address where he is living at?" She said, "Mr. Woodard do you mean to tell me that he is not living at the address that he is registered to?" I said, "Yes, he lives with my Ex-Wife." She then told me to excuse her for a few minutes. She called over to the Sex Offender Unit and left a message. She then told me that I would be getting a phone call the next day.

The following day I received a phone call in the morning from the head of the Sex Offender Department at the Sheriff's Office. The Deputy told me that she knew there was something going on with this guy and that I was the missing piece to the puzzle. She explained the rules that Sex Offenders have to abide by in order to stay within compliance of their probation. One of those rules was the fact that if they have three consecutive overnight stays at the same address, they must register that as their address. It's public knowledge and that neighborhood has the right to know that there is a sexual predator living in the area. She said, "We have been looking for Wendell for quite some time." Every three months they would have to verify all sexual predators at their residence. It had been about six months since they could verify Wendell at his Mom's home. Court documents say, that the Sheriff's Department thought that Wendell's Mom and Sister, who lived at his registered address were covering for him and telling him when the deputy would stop by so that he could return for verification. She kept his file on her desk even though they verified him. She told me that she got a complaint from Mary months ago saying that I passed out flyers in her neighborhood that had information on it about her and Wendell. I didn't even know she was trying to get me into trouble with the law until now. The police kept the flyer that she brought them on February 15, 2010. Apparently the proof that she brought the police to get me into trouble was evidence that would backfire against her according to an article written in the local newspaper the Fayetteville Observer on July 15, 2011. The Deputy interviewed Dante', Jordan, Chrissy and me and I gave them copies of all the documents that I had on Wendell. I also showed them the pictures that I took of his car late at night months ago at her home. The deputy told me that his ex-girlfriend lived in the same neighborhood and she was bitter, but didn't want to say too much about him when questioned. She suspected the ex-girlfriend as being the one that handed those flyers out around the neighborhood. She then told me that they have two warrants for his arrest and due to the fact that he had a history with guns and drugs, they were passing this on to the U.S. Marshall's office to handle the arrest. She told me that someone would be in touch.

Two days later I was contacted by the U.S. Marshall's office. They asked me a ton of questions and I cooperated as much as I could. I knew this was the right way to handle this situation given the fact that I could of went to jail for physically harming this guy for putting his hands on my Son. They told me that they staked out the house the last couple of days and he is in fact living there. He has spent the night and he comes and goes normally. They told me that I could not tell anyone about this investigation so that I don't jeopardize the arrest. The following morning was a Wednesday morning and the kids were coming to my house. The U.S. Marshall's were outside of her house waiting until they made their move. They called me when the garage door opened. I told them that she was coming to drop the kids off at my house. They wanted me to call them when she was returning. I asked why they needed to know when she was returning. They said, "Because we have a warrant for her arrest as well." My mouth dropped. I still didn't know what she did. I called them when she dropped the kids off and let them know that she was on the way and I was told that they would call me later. About an hour and half had past so I called to find out what was going on. The Marshall answered his phone and told me that both Wendell and Mary had been arrested at their home. He said after she returned they waited another 20 minutes and the garage door opened up again. At that time they swarmed the home and made the arrest without incident. Mary's Mom was still staying with them as well so the Marshall's had to secure the perimeter and pat her down as well.

So here are the hard facts concerning this situation. According to court documents, Wendell was arrested and charged with failing to register his address and living less than 1,000 feet from a Day Care. According to her arrest warrant that I obtained, Mary was arrested and charged with harboring a sex offender and failing to notify authorities. He was in jail being held with a $51,000 secured bond and she was released after paying a $5,000 bond later that day. What am I going to tell the kids? That's what went through my head at that time. I got home from work that day and the kids and I were sitting in the living room when the news came on. The story about their arrest was on the news. The kids now saw this story on TV. I sat them down and told them what happened. I was expecting to have to comfort them, but to my surprise my Son Dante's reaction was, "She knew she was doing wrong and she got what she deserved." I couldn't believe that after all this time, they felt this way about what happened. I viewed a sense of relief on their faces and a sorrowful look for their Mom. The next day I went to see an attorney and we filed for custody once again. This time my attorney filed for an "Ex Parte." This is a Latin legal term meaning on one side only. My attorney met with the Judge and presented our case without Mary's side of the story in order for me to have custody of the kids until the temporary custody hearing. The order was signed and custody was given to me. The hearing wasn't for three weeks. That Friday, when I got home from work, the boys and I hopped in the car after packing and drove to Tampa, FL to visit Chrissy and get out of Fayetteville. I didn't want them around all of the mess that was going on. We took them everywhere they wanted to go and just spoiled them so that they could enjoy being kids. They were to have no contact with their Mom and I explained this to them very delicately. As the third week approached my attorney said that she agreed with Mary's attorney to allow the kids to communicate with Mary over the phone. I let them speak with her and they didn't have much to say. As a Father who has handled this entire situation the correct way, I felt that this should now be an open and shut case. The Judge told her to keep Wendell away from the kids, they both were arrested and charged with felony crimes, Mary actually took the police the evidence they needed to warrant her arrest. The flyer that she took the police on

February 15, 2011 had Wendell's registered address on it and other personal information according to court documents. Therefore, she knew that he was registered at his Mom's house and she moved him in anyway without notifying the authorities. I was expecting to get full custody of the kids that day, but I found out just how unjust the court system can be on technicalities. My attorney presented her case. It was strong, to the point and we had hard facts to back up our story. When the Judge rendered her verdict she said to my attorney, "I agree with everything you said and admire your client for handling the situation like he did, but since your client knew the status of Wendell Jones at the time the parenting agreement was signed at mediation and he didn't put in a provision to keep him away from the kids, I am going to restore the parenting agreement for visitation purposes and give shared custody until the final hearing. I was absolutely devastated! I could not believe what I just heard. The Judge was under the impression that I went into mediation and never said anything about Wendell being around my kids. She wasn't aware of the first mediation when I started off the conversation saying, "I don't want Wendell Smith around my kids", it was a technicality that hurt me at the worst possible time. I had to deal with what the Judge said. What a trying time for the kids, myself and Chrissy. After this occurred yet a second time, I lost all trust in Mary. She chose a man, a sex offender over her kids and I can't explain to you how upsetting this was for me. Her true colors were now exposed. Many people saw this. I was told that she upset some of her family members after lying about breaking up with Wendell in order to borrow money for an attorney. In the following months, things continued to get worse. My kids were caught up in all of the chaos and disrespect that went on in her household. I made the decision that it was time for me to move. Chrissy and I were getting married on September 10, 2011 and it was good timing for me to remove myself from this situation so that my kids could have some peace. The plan was to get full custody of them and then move to Tampa, but I had to leave the kids behind. However, Dante' did everything he could in order to move to Tampa with Chrissy and me. Finally in early January, Dante' was arguing with his Mom and he called me and asked for me to come get him. She signed the paper work for him to move and he has been with Chrissy and me ever since. I never wanted to split up the boys, but Mary would not let Jordan move with us. Let me just explain how I felt when I was in the courtroom. I saw father after father after father go up and give away their rights to their children just so they didn't have to deal with the mother anymore. I could not believe it. Many black father's at that. I was highly upset and offended. Here I am, in court fighting to protect my kids, and these guys just signed off relinquishing their rights to their kids. Father's going into a custody case already are on the losing end in my opinion. This is what I faced during this process. To sum it up, on the criminal side of things according to court documents, Wendell spent about 19 months in jail after he pled guilty to the charges brought against him and he got out on time served. The assault charge was dismissed since he would have received a sentence of time served for that charge as well. Mary pled guilty to a lesser charge in order to avoid any additional jail time. She pled guilty to a charge called, "Misprison of a Felony." The definition of that is, *"Whoever, having knowledge of the actual commission of a felony, conceals and does not as soon as possible make known the same to some judge or other person in civil or military authority under the United States" is guilty of misprision of felony and can be punished up to three years in prison*. Even though things didn't work out entirely the way I wanted them to, I still believe that I handled it the right way, which was through the court system and not by street justice. If I can do it fellas, you can as well.

Fighting for Custody Key Points

- Men stop giving up so easy. You have just as much right to be a good father as the woman has to be a good mother.

- Step up to the plate and handle your responsibilities. The children didn't ask to be put in this situation.

- Always do what's in the best interest of the kids. Even if that means sacrificing your own feelings.

- No matter what you go through never lose sight of the fact that your kids are your top priority.

- Never put a man or woman above your kids.

- Take your time introducing a man or woman to your kids because if things don't work out and you break up, your children will now have to suffer breaking up as well.

- Before you bring a significant other around your kids, make sure that a thorough background check is completed.

- Go through the court system and handle things the right way so that each agreed upon rule is legally documented.

Marrying My Best Friend

CHRISSY AND I PLANNED on getting married on September 10, 2011. Yes that is 9/10/11. It is so crazy that it worked out that way. It was also the one year anniversary of our engagement. 9/10/10. Fellas I can never go wrong from here on out since I have one of the easiest Anniversaries to remember. All of the planning for our special day started right after we got engaged. The hardest decisions were finding a location and deciding what city we wanted to have the Wedding Ceremony in. At this time I was still living in Fayetteville, NC, Chrissy was in Tampa, FL and both of our families lived in Pennsylvania. Decisions, decisions! We knew that the venue was the most important thing to secure so we did a ton of searching at this time. We originally thought about having the Ceremony and the Reception at the Pittsburgh Aquarium. Then we had second thoughts about that because of the inconvenient travel time for all of our guests. We then decided to look at having it in Erie, PA since the majority of my family lives there. I started making some calls and checking venues for availability and I was able to secure the Ambassador Center at the Hilton Garden Inn for the ceremony and the Erie Yacht was chosen for the Reception. It was all coming together. I did the majority of the planning since I grew up in Erie and had more knowledge of the area. We wanted this day to be perfect. We knew who we wanted to represent us in the wedding so we began to make phone calls and shared our news with our future Bridesmaids and Groomsmen. Everyone was so happy for us. I chose one of my Best Friends to be my Best Man. I asked Otha Davidson and he gladly accepted. We also needed a Pastor to marry us and I had been good friends with Bishop Clifton McNair. Our families have known each other for years. He and is wonderful Wife Richarda McNair were co-pastors at their own church called the Word of Life Christian Center International. It is a wonderful Nondenominational Church in Erie so I asked him if he would officiate the Ceremony and he said he would be honored to. It all started to fall into place from that point on. We were coming to Pennsylvania for Thanksgiving and we were able to go to the Erie County Courthouse and apply for our Marriage License, we had an appointment at the Ambassador Center to see the hall where the ceremony would take place and we also made arrangements to go to the Erie Yacht Club and look around as well as pick out our options from the menu. This was such a fun time for us.

When we got back home to Fayetteville and Tampa, Chrissy and I began to get our guest list together. We wanted to invite as many people as we could, but it just wasn't feasible to do so financially. We had to come up with a number and stick to that number since we were paying for the wedding ourselves. This was challenging, but we came up with a number and completed our list. Next I had to secure a DJ for the music, a videographer, a photographer and order the Limo. A good friend of mine, Curtis Jones AKA The Captain, was the first person that came to mind. I called him up and asked if he was available that date and he was willing to make himself available. I had already asked one of my best friends, Jeff Sansom, to be in the wedding and he said yes and told me not to worry about getting anyone to record the wedding. He did this for a living and he said he would take care of it for me. What a gift that was. I thought about asking my cousin Larry Moyer to be the photographer. I called him up and checked on his availability and he said he would shoot our wedding as well. The last piece of the puzzle I needed was a Limo. I contacted Rupp Limousine and asked them about 9/10/11 and they were able to squeeze us in on that day. This was perfect. All I wanted Chrissy to have to worry about was picking out her dress. I went to the Men's Warehouse to look for the tuxedos the fellas and I were going to wear. The colors that Chrissy and I came up with were Black, White and Red. All of the guys were set to wear all Black tuxedos with a Red Rose, the Bridesmaids were going to wear all Black Dresses with Red Roses, Dante' and Jordan had White Tuxedos with Black pin stripes and Chrissy and I were going to wear all White with Red Roses. We could just imagine how that would look. The symbol we chose to have throughout our wedding theme was the double hearts. We found beautiful invitations with the double hearts on them and I put them all together and mailed out every last one of them. It was exciting getting the RSVP's back and creating our final guest list. Chrissy and I had to go out and purchase a lot of the extras that go along with a wedding. That was pretty fun to do. We picked out the cake at Giant Eagle and they made a beautiful cake for us and Karen, Chrissy's Mom, had Chrissy's Rose Arrangement made. It was all coming together nicely.

Chrissy flew to Raleigh, NC and the boys and I picked her up from the airport. We then got our tuxedos and we were ready for our trip to Pennsylvania. We drove up to Kittanning a few days prior to the Rehearsal Dinner to relax before our weekend began. We had a block of rooms set aside for those coming from out of town at the Comfort Inn. Early Friday morning, September 9, 2011, we all were ready to leave Karen and Robert's house and head to Erie to get settled into the hotel and get ready for the rehearsal dinner. By mid-afternoon we made it to our rooms. I met Otha in Erie and I stayed with him at the Ambassador that night so that I wouldn't see Chrissy until she started walking down the aisle on Saturday. Everything was going as planned. We all met at the Ambassador and did our walk through. I could just envision how everything would look. We had the rehearsal dinner at Oscar's Pub that night and the food was fantastic. The entire wedding party and those who came in from out of town were present and we had such a fun time that night. After the dinner the wedding party, along with Chrissy and I, went out to socialize. We went to an old spot of mine owned by a good friend, Johnny's Sports Bar. I had known Johnny Bizzarro and his family for years and did Sports Features on most of the Bizzarro's for Boxing. He took care of us that night and we had a blast. Now it was time to say goodbye. Chrissy was leaving with the ladies and Otha and I were headed back to the Ambassador. The next time I would see her would be moments before she was named Mrs. Woodard. I gave her a big hug and kiss and we shed a tear or two and went our respective ways. The next morning I hooked up with Khyl Horton after picking up Dante' and Jordan from my Mom's house and we went to go get our haircuts. After that, I stopped up at the Ambassador to see what needed to be done setting up the room. I then stopped at the Mall to buy Dante' and Jordan a gift to present to them during the ceremony. We thought that it would be very special to do a "Joining of the Children" segment during the ceremony. This was actually Chrissy's idea. Since I had children to a prior marriage, this would make it symbolic for the boys and I to accept Chrissy into our family and for Chrissy to accept all of us as one. It was very special. Chrissy was having a tough time on her end. She had to get her hair done and the hairdresser was taking so long to complete her hair. She was running late and had issues with her dress then to add insult to injury, the Limo driver went to the wrong hotel to pick her up. That pushed the wedding back even further, however God is good and he smiled upon us that day. The ceremony began and Bishop McNair led Otha, Dante', Jordan and me into the room. The wedding party began to proceed down the aisle. I forgot to mention that we would be one person short. Chrissy's good friend Jennifer Daubman Byerly was a bridesmaid, but she was pregnant and expecting any day and she lived in Pittsburgh so she was unable to attend the wedding. Pastor Richarda McNair took her place and made sure that we didn't skip a beat. In comes the party. Everyone looks so good. I was filled with a range of emotions. I was happy, nervous and amazed at all of the love I felt in that room. I'm an emotional person at heart and I'm man enough to share my emotions with others. That has never bothered me, so when the doors opened in the back and Chrissy stood with her Stepfather Robert Erdley I just lost it. She looked so beautiful and reality set in. This was the day, it was finally here. I began to cry as my heart filled with joy and love. Each step she got closer to me and closer until finally Robert, AKA Pap, handed her off to me. Wow she was so beautiful. The dress she chose was stunning! I could not believe that this was going to be my Wife. God blessed me with a second chance and at this moment it was so surreal. We did the lighting of the candles, the joining of the children and we got right to our vows. Then the words I had been waiting to hear for so long came out. "By the powers vested in me by the Commonwealth of Pennsylvania, I now pronounce you man and wife. Craig you may kiss your bride." We DID IT! I was the happiest man on earth. As we walked down the end of the aisle for a picture. The happy looks on our faces were priceless. I had married my best friend. The ceremony ended up being just as beautiful. The dinner was excellent, the view in the back by the water of the sunset was incredible and we were blessed to be amongst family and friends. My Aunt Bettie read a poem for us along with a great friend of mine Dayne Bailey. Dayne and Christy's daughter Shaye is my God Daughter so it was very special to us to have them read on our special day.

We asked my father to say a few words at the reception. He spoke about life, success and family and his words were so moving. We all shared a special moment when he wrapped up. I hugged my Dad and I cried my eyes out, Chrissy came up and she cried as well. My Mother joined us and we all cried together. What this moment symbolized for us was the fact that we were welcoming a major addition to our family. Chrissy was now a Wife, a daughter-in-law, and a Stepmother. She took on these roles just by saying I do. The strength she has given me and the boys during such a trying time was all generated from the love that she had for me for close to 20 years. My Mom and Dad knew who I had by my side and they grew very close to her. What a great moment in my life.

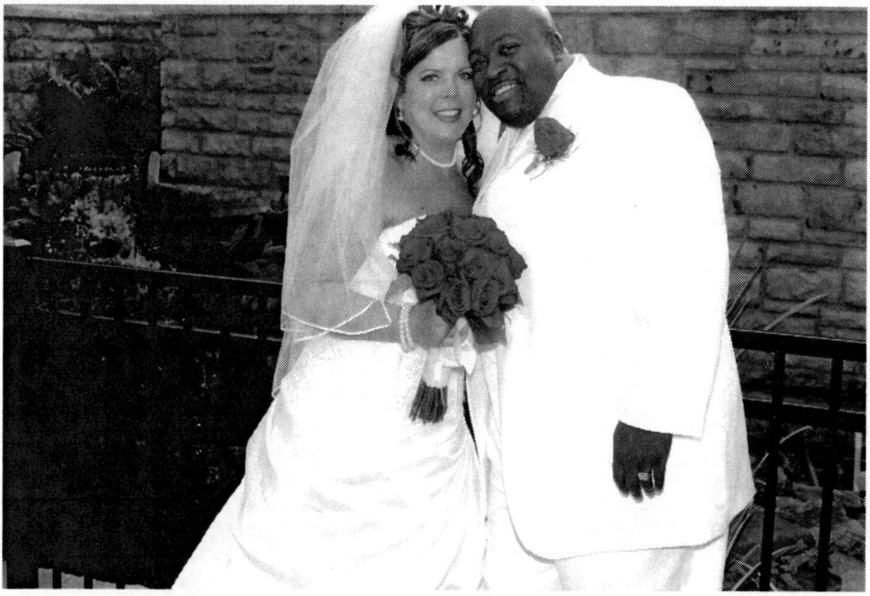

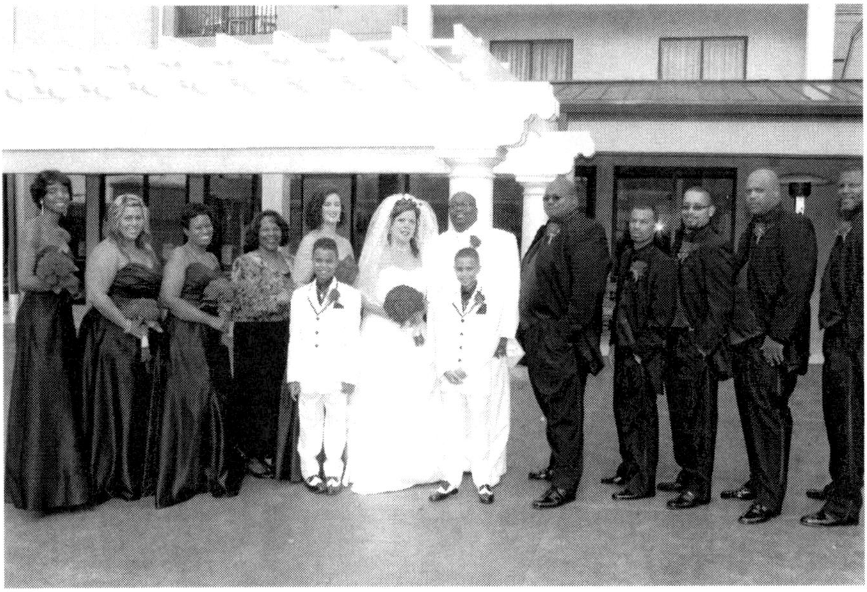

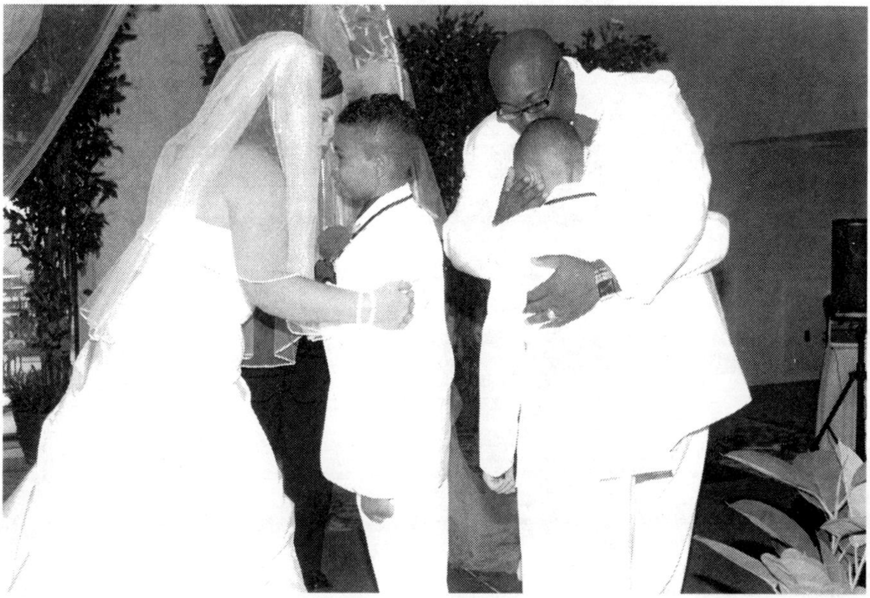

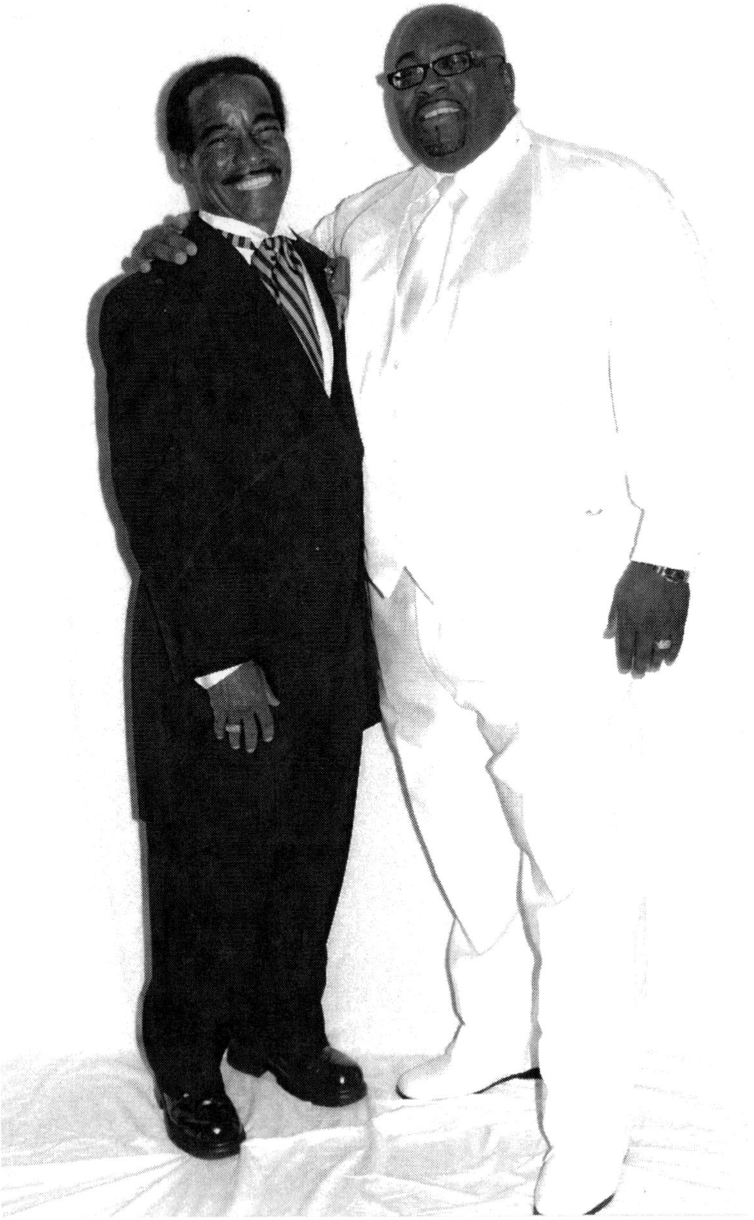

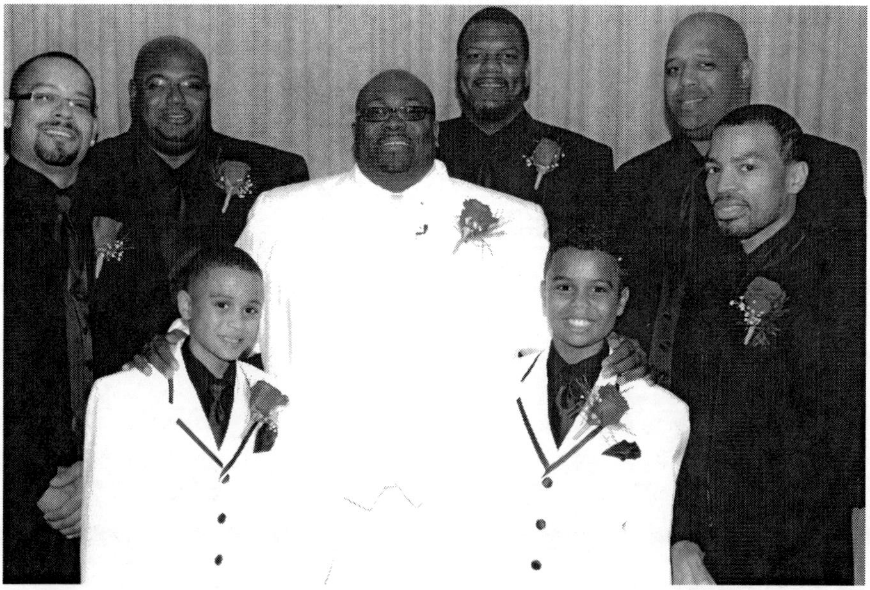

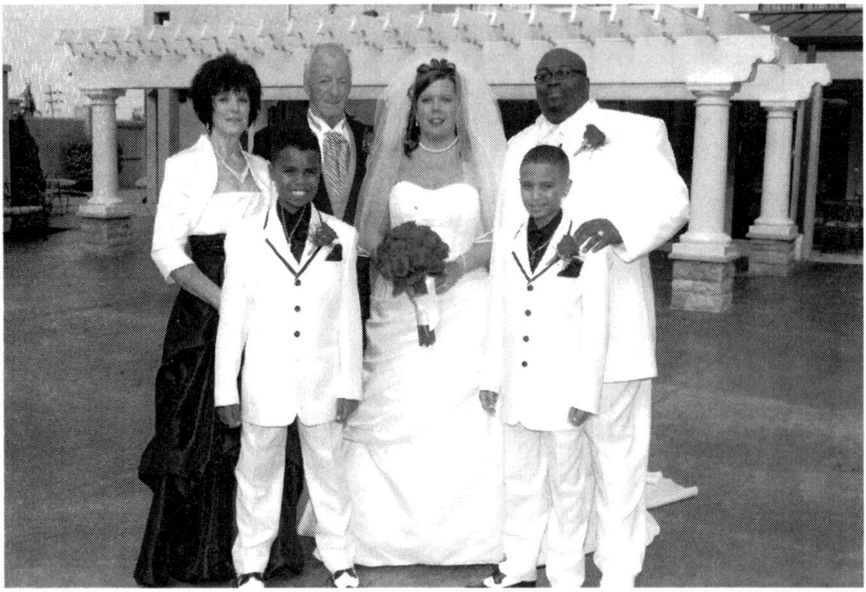

Marrying My Best Friend Key Points

- When God places that chosen one in front of you, make sure that you preserve your relationship.

- Become friends first and lovers second.

- Don't ever go to sleep angry at one another.

- Fellas be gentlemen and treat your lady very special. Chivalry is not dead. Open doors for your woman at all times. You'll find that the women of the other guys who don't do this will look at your woman with jealous eyes. Women notice everything. That in itself makes your woman feel extra special. Trust me. I have done this for my Wife from day one.

- Be prepared to say I'm sorry and mean it.

- Winning every argument is no longer important. Respecting each other's opinion is.

- Choose your arguments wisely. Don't sweat the small stuff.

Junior's Journey

A MONTH AFTER CHRISSY and I got married back in 2011, I finally transferred with my job from Fayetteville, NC to Tampa, FL as District Manager for Springleaf Financial Services in the middle of October. I moved in with Chrissy in a small two bedroom apartment. We had the greatest time there. We started talking about having a baby. Chrissy didn't have any children of her own so she wanted to have a baby. In January 2012 we were blessed with the best news ever. Chrissy took a pregnancy test and it came back positive. She took another one and showed it to me and that one was positive as well. We were so excited. She called her doctor and scheduled an appointment so that we could make this official. Here we are newlyweds and we were going to be brand new parents. We started to think about all of the different baby names we would choose from. We tried to keep this a secret until we confirmed the news with the doctor, but we told a few people. I told only four people, my Dad, my Mom, and two of my closest friends Jeff and Otha. Chrissy told her Mom and Stepdad. Chrissy had already started getting morning sickness. She had it real bad. One night she had to go to the emergency room because she became dehydrated. At this time, Dante' had already come to live with us. He was in the 6th grade. He was very excited about the news as well. A couple of weeks went by before our doctor's appointment and the entire time Chrissy was struggling with morning sickness. I don't even know if I want to call it morning sickness anymore because she was sick morning, noon and night. Finally the day had come and we went to see the doctor. They did a pregnancy test and it came back positive so then did an ultrasound and determined that she was roughly eight weeks pregnant. When doing the ultrasound, the nurse left the room and brought the doctor back. We didn't understand what was going on. They finally said they saw the embryo, but it didn't look like it was developing correctly in the yolk sac. They told us that we may have miscarried. Our world came crashing down. We couldn't take this news. My Wife's first child and we received news like this. It was heartbreaking. The doctor told us to come back in two days and she would do another ultrasound. When we arrived they performed another ultrasound and this time we saw the yolk sac and there was a heartbeat detected. She gave us the good news, but also let us know that the heartbeat was very faint. We scheduled another appointment for the following Monday and at this appointment there was no heartbeat detected at all. We had lost our baby. Chrissy and I were devastated. We held each other tightly and cried in the office. She had to now schedule a D&C. This was a dilation and curettage, a surgical procedure to open up the cervix and remove the contents of the uterus. We had to wait a few months before attempted to try to get pregnant again after this procedure was complete. This was a tough time in our lives, but we kept our faith in the Lord. We stopped thinking about getting pregnant and just operated by the, "If it happens, it happens," concept.

About a year and half later, in the summer of 2013, Chrissy took another pregnancy test. Surprised again when it came back positive. We had been through this before so we didn't want to get over excited. We called and set up an appointment with the doctor. When the appointment came, the doctor did the test and confirmed not only our pregnancy, but the fact that the baby had a strong heartbeat. What a relief. The doctor then made sure that we were sent over to another medical facility due to Chrissy being considered high risk due to her age. So we had many appointments to go to and it was extremely nerve racking. In October of 2013 we had an ultrasound performed and some additional testing done. When the results came back, the doctor advised us that there is a chance that our child could have Down Syndrome. We never expected this so we took this very hard. He asked us if we wanted to have an Amniocentesis done and he explained the risks of this procedure. An Amniocentesis is a procedure where they insert a needle into the womb and withdraw some of the amniotic fluid. Then they test the amniotic fluid to see if the baby has certain genetic or chromosomal abnormality such as Down Syndrome. Chrissy was about 17 weeks pregnant at this time so we decided that we would want to find out earlier than later. The outcome didn't matter since we decided that we were going to keep our child anyway. We just wanted to know if he had it or not. The sex of the baby had already been determined, we already knew we were having a boy. I knew at that point I wanted to name my son Craig Woodard, Jr. We decided to proceed with the Amniocentesis. It didn't take very long to do, but we were very nervous. We were hoping that the baby wouldn't be as active when the doctor was inserting the needle into the womb. The doctor was very gentle and very quick and the procedure was a success. He ran the results on the fluid and it came back positive for Down Syndrome. Again, we took this news very hard. This was not an easy thing to go through. Chrissy was just as sick during this pregnancy as she was the first time she got pregnant. We began to do a ton of research on Down Syndrome and the quality of life our child would have. There was hope that the test results were a false positive and he didn't have Down Syndrome. We prayed and cried and asked the Lord to guide us through this tough time. During some of the future visits, we found out that Craig Jr. had fluid on his brain and he was starting to have heart issues. Every time we left the doctor's office we shed tears for our son. We were referred to a Cardiologist and this doctor told us exactly what was wrong and what he thought would happen. He told us that there was a Coarctation of the Aorta. This was a narrowing in the aortic arch which slowed the amount of blood flow to the body and to the brain. He said if the narrowing closes they would have to do surgery to open it. He said if it remains the same, they may just have to monitor it as he grows older. He said, his opinion was that the arch would continue to grow wider as he grew older. That was somewhat of a relief, but this was only an opinion.

They scheduled an inducement for Chrissy the day she entered into her 39th week. We were having stress tests done all of the time in order to monitor the baby. Chrissy was scheduled to go to the hospital on Sunday April 13, 2014 and they were going to induce her that night with hopes she would deliver on Monday April 14th. The prior Friday, April 12th, we had a stress test scheduled. During the stress test the baby's activity wasn't as busy as usual. Our kick count was very low. The nurse sent a sound wave to the baby to wake him up and that worked. He must have been sleeping when we were getting the stress test down, but Chrissy and I wondered about that. We went home and tried to enjoy the weekend. We were very excited and anxious for Sunday to roll around. Finally the day was here. April 13, 2014. I had her bag packed and drove her down to the hospital at 2:55 pm. We were giving birth at St. Joseph's Hospital. The ironic thing was that I was born in Flint, Michigan at St. Joseph's Hospital. I thought that was very cool. We checked in at St. Joe's and they took us back and immediately started a stress test. All was going well until the nurse kept having Chrissy turn from side to side. She had her turn close to ten times and then she left the room and went to get the doctor. They hadn't starting inducing her as of yet, but we looked at each other and thought something was wrong. Chrissy began to stress and she started to cry. I comforted her the best way a loving husband could, but it didn't seem to help. The doctor came in and looked at the monitor and said we need to take the baby. Prepare for a Caesarean Section. They went into emergency mode and we knew that every second counted. Before I could even kiss my Wifey goodbye, they rushed her away and they were giving me clothing to put on so I could be in there with her. I lost all communication with my Mother-in-law back in Pennsylvania. I was keeping her posted by updating her via text. I put on my hospital gear and they took me into the surgery room. Chrissy began to get sick on the surgery table. I sat there and kept her head tilted sideways so that she wouldn't choke. They began the Caesarean Section. This was happening so fast. They told me when I could stand up to look over the sheet they had up as a barrier. When I stood up I saw them pull Craig Jr. out and cut his umbilical cord. They handed him off to Dr. Foster, who was the Head of the Neonatal Unit and she took him over to the corner out of sight. All of a sudden we heard cry out in order to take his first breath. There was a sigh of relief, until we heard them say he had a collapsed lung. I was able to take a quick picture of him then they rushed him up to the neonatal unit. Chrissy was doing okay, I gave her a big kiss and they took me out of the surgery room while they finished with Chrissy. I then went and got all of our stuff and went to the lobby to let everyone know what was going on. About 30 minutes past and I went back to the nurse and asked what room she was going to be in. I took our stuff up there and met Chrissy in the recovery room. I told her everything that was going on. We walked into the hospital at 2:55 pm and Craig Jr. was born 6 lbs. 11 oz. at 5:52 pm. Less than 3 hours.

It was amazing. I had to wait for Chrissy to get the feeling back in her legs before they could send her upstairs to her room. Chrissy's room was on the 5th floor and Craig Jr's room was on the 2nd. Finally we got upstairs and I made sure Chrissy was okay and she was settled in. I then rushed downstairs to Craig Jr's room and Dr. Foster and some of the nurses were in there. I introduced myself to all of them and they filled me in on his progress. What I saw tore my heart out. Since he had a collapsed lung, they had him under what's called an Oxy Hood. This was supposed to help his lung inflate. They also had intravenous line in his arm and he had blood pressure cuffs on his arm and leg. He underwent phototherapy and had a cover on his eyes because they said he was jaundice. All I prayed for was that our child would be okay. It was a sight to see. I knew he had a long road ahead of him, but now I was thinking of how I could tell Chrissy while keeping her emotionally intact. Remember, she hadn't seen him yet or held him.

I stayed in Craig Jr's room for about two hours. I was able to hold him when he was just a couple of hours old. To me he was perfect, but it killed me seeing our son attached to all of those wires and cords. I said goodbye to Junior and went back upstairs to check on Chrissy and give her an update. I was planning on spending the night at the hospital for at least two days. I got back to her room and she was in a lot of pain. I told her how well she did and how much I loved her. I thanked her for doing such an incredible job and for giving me Craig Jr. We had a very special moment. I then began to tell her what was going on with Junior. I asked her if she felt up to going to visit him. She said she couldn't because she was in way too much pain. I told her to try to get as much rest as she could. She shut her eyes and fell asleep pretty quickly. I was exhausted as well so I fell asleep. I woke up in the middle of the night and I went downstairs to see Junior. I brought his milk down so that they could store it in the refrigerator since Chrissy was pumping in order to breast feed. Every few hours I would go check on Junior. The following morning Chrissy felt stronger and I put her in a wheel chair and took her to see our boy. She was so excited and scared at the same time. She cried when we got into his room and I'm sure she felt the same way I did when I first saw him connected to all of those wires and cords. She spent a good amount of time down in his room and it was very nice to be together finally. Later in the day we got some visitors. My Mom came, Karen and Pap drove down from Kittanning and they came to see him, I went home and picked up Dante' and brought him back, our nephew Dillon came to the hospital as well and then two good friends of ours, Chrissy's two co-workers Ashley Phelps and Suzanne Madden came to see him.

Every day he continued to get better and better. By Monday evening they had removed him from phototherapy. We could finally see his eyes. They checked his heart condition daily by doing Echocardiograms. Chrissy was in the hospital until that Thursday April 17th and then she was released. It was hard taking her home knowing that Craig Jr. had to stay in the Neonatal Unit for a bit longer. On Sunday morning we received a wonderful call from the doctor. She told us that Craig Jr's PDA closed in his heart. The PDA is the Patent Ductus Ateriosus. This is the normal hole in the heart that typically closes a few days after birth. However, it remains open with some babies, but Craig Jr's closed and they wanted to see how that would affect the narrowing of the Aortic Arch. The good news is that nothing happened. His arch remained the same which led the doctors to believe that it will not get any narrower and it may open wider over time. She said if Junior passes his vision and hearing tests and the car seat check then he can go home sometime on Monday. You guessed it, I broke down in tears again. This time hearing that his heart was going to be okay just floored me. I prayed so hard for Junior and the good Lord answered my prayers. We went and got Junior and brought him home on Monday April 20, 2014. It was nice having him home. We had a number of doctor appointments and follow ups to go through, but each time we went he continued to get good results. The genetics Doctor did a physical exam on Junior while he was in the hospital and she did officially diagnose him with Down Syndrome, but it didn't matter to us. We have a special gift from God and he is a wonderful little boy. God wouldn't give us more than what we could handle.

While Craig Jr.'s journey is progressing, I was in the middle of serving on the Grand Jury. I served from the first week in January

2014 – the last Thursday in June 2014. Six months of service and this was considered the highest form of community service. We met almost every Thursday as needed and our job was to decide if the state presented enough evidence in order for us to indict the suspect and send the case to trial for First Degree Murder. We heard testimony and saw evidence from lead police detectives, forensic pathologists and even Medical Examiners that performed autopsies on the deceased. We saw crime scene photos and autopsy pictures that you would never ever see on television. It was so depressing. This chapter in my life put everything in perspective for me. Seeing all of the death and how all of these murders were committed made me more aware of how I can protect my family. With a newborn, a new wife and two other kids, my job as a father and husband was clear. I cherished every moment that our family spent with each other and I still do. I was taught that you must live life like there is no tomorrow. Also don't sweat the small stuff because tomorrow is not promised to you. The protection I have for my family has grown since this experience and with the birth of Craig Jr., I now have a new outlook on life. Junior has challenges that he must overcome, but there are other families out there who have lost their loved ones. God doesn't give us more than what we can handle. Just always be prepared to handle as much as you can.

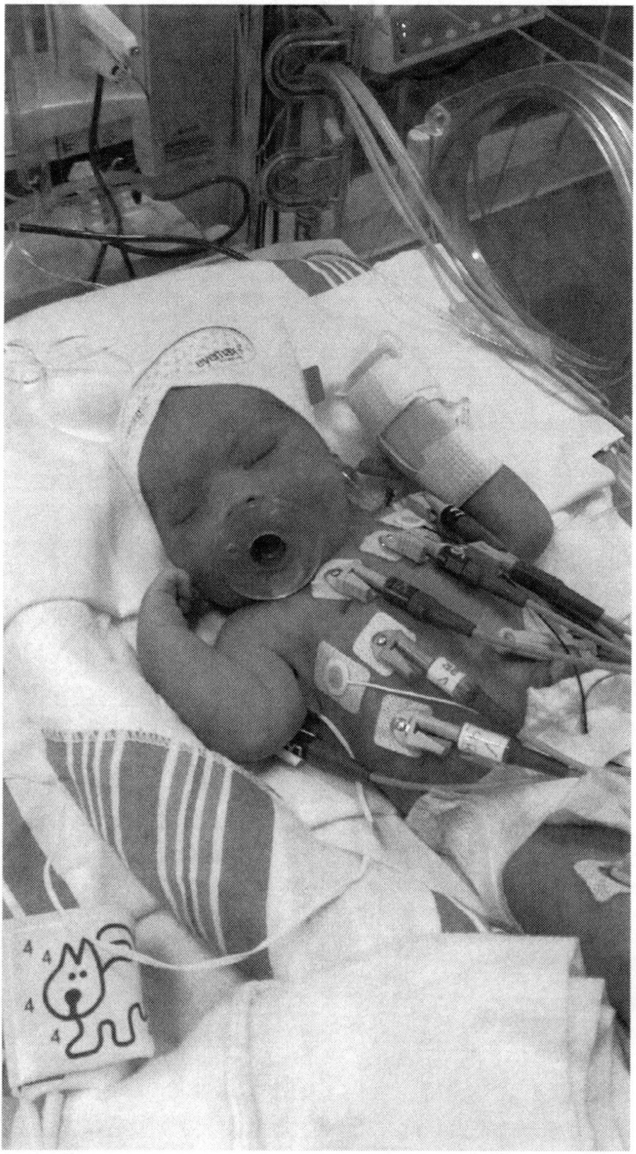

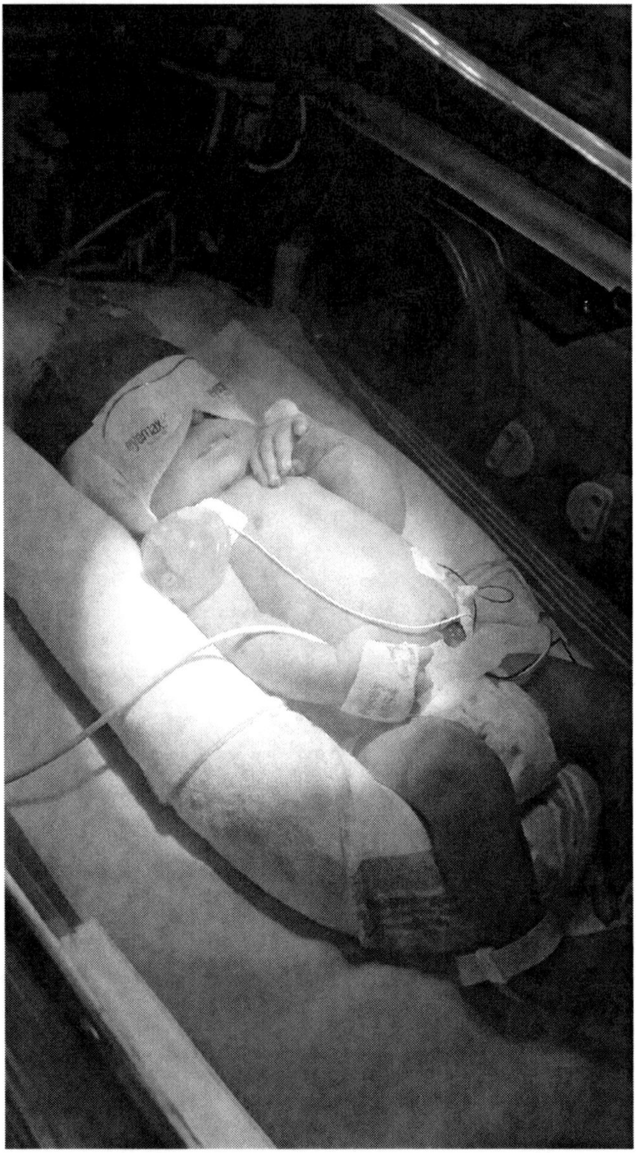

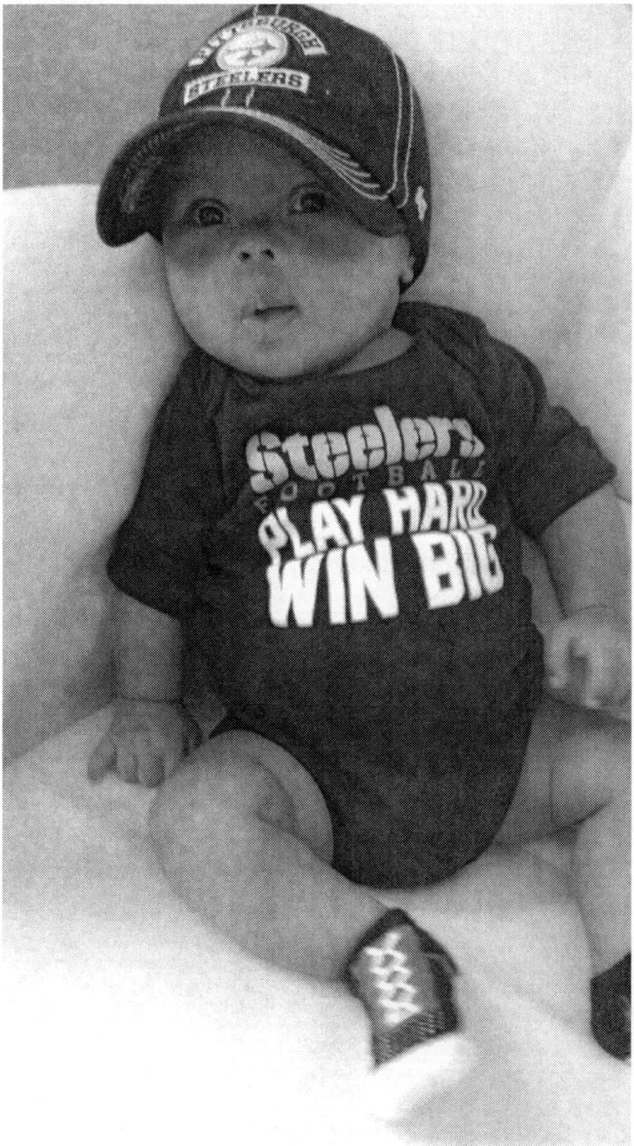
STEELERS
Steelers
FOOTBALL
PLAY HARD
WIN BIG

Junior's Journey Key Points

- Love your children unconditionally.

- Put your children in God's hands and trust that he will never forsaken you.

- Raise your children to have respect.

- Teach them to be independent.

- Show them by example how to conduct themselves in public.

- Be affectionate with your kids. Always kiss and hug them no matter how old they get.

- Tell them you love them daily.

- Believe that God has a plan for your child. Be supportive of them when they express an interest in something even if it's not interesting to you.

- I'm a firm believer in the saying, "Spare the rod, spoil the child."

- Live life to the fullest.

My life has been 40 years of a series of unique events. Everyone lives similar yet different lives. I grew up in two separate loving households after going through the adjustments of my parents getting divorced. I lived with both of them and experienced how each parent handled being a single parent. I matured and grew into a young man who wanted my own identity. I made some important decisions throughout my life and I made some decisions that I regret as well. However you look at it, this is my life and my moments and I wanted to share them with you in order to educate, encourage, and to let many of our young folks know that you can face trials and tribulations and still make something of yourselves. You can come from a broken home and still become a success. You can bring children into an imperfect world and still be the model parent and great role model that you desire to be. All it takes is effort, hard work, determination and tenacity. If you have the desire to want to win in life, you will keep the hunger for the taste of success.

There have been way too many shootings and killings in my hometown over the last couple of years and many young black males have lost their lives. I have challenged many of my good male friends and/or fathers on social media for 2015. The challenge is called, "Each One, Teach One." I have challenged many men to make sure they enlighten, empower and teach a young black male something about life and success when they come in contact with them. We can make a change. If we touch just one we have done our job. I challenged them and they all accepted. Together we will save our future. WE'RE A MOVEMENT BY OURSELVES, BUT WE'RE A FORCE WHEN WE'RE TOGETHER! EACH ONE, TEACH ONE!

Thank you for wanting to learn a little bit more about my life and my family and if I motivate someone or give someone the strength to make it through a similar situation, then writing this autobiography was well worth it. God bless you all.

Acknowledgments

I spent man many hours writing my first book and this took valuable time away from my family. Having a newborn on hand made it even that much more difficult. For that I want to say thank you to my Wifey, Christine Woodard, you gave up your time with me in order to let me be creative. You let me share myself with whoever reads my book. You were the first person that I told one Saturday morning that I was going to write an Autobiography. Chrissy you are a great Mother, Stepmother and Wife and I thank you for inspiring me to be the best that I can be. I think you all can see how much Chrissy did for the kids and me. It took a special person to not only stay with me through much of the turmoil that I went through with my ex-wife, but to also take in my children as her own and want to protect them throughout the proceedings. Chrissy I could not have made it through life without you. I credit you for keeping me calm and focused and out of jail. You Wifey are my rock, my best friend and I thank and love you from the bottom of my heart.

I want to also thank my Mother in Law and Father in Law Karen and Robert (Pap) Erdley. I love you two very much and thank you for always being there for me. Also to my Grandmother Chris Kirkemier. You are the best and I love you with all my heart. Thank you for being you!

I would like to thank all of the Coaches I have had in my life that pushed me to be the best. Walter Soboleski, John Purvis, Al Metrik, Greg Majchrzak, Al Rush, Ron Costello, Michael Allen, Dan Rosenburg, Jim Chapman, Joe Kimball, Armand Rocco Jr., Dave Curtis, Dave Armstrong, Bob Nuber, Yvonne Parker, Carl Crennel, and Gary Tufford. I thank you all.

I would like to thank all of my teammates that helped me accomplish the accolades I was able to achieve. I was on many teams throughout my career so it will be hard to name every single teammate, but I do want to acknowledge a few. Keith Pulliam, Mike King, Luke Purvis, Shawn and John Warner, Mark Soboleski, Chris James, Tony Robie, Khyl Horton, Jeff Sansom, Shelby Wiley, Freddie Jones, Brian Wedzik,

Brian Dahlkemper, Chris Logero, Matt Golga, Dayne Bailey, Matthew Hatchette, Ryan Banks, Chris Vlasic, Bill Davis, , Jason Myers, Brian Dloniak, Chris Soltis, Brian Burton, Rafael Cooper, Anthony Campoli Jr., Dave Seyboldt, Brian O'Hara, Mike Uhler, Jared Lawrie, Chris Kessler, Dan and Ed Regovich, Bronze Simpson, Mike Vaughn, Tim Cook, Gerald Battle, Jody Dickerson, Michael Parker Sr., Otha Davidson, Kevin Williams, Carmen Williams, Mike Peck, Shea Berkley, Reggie Blanchard, Mike DiBartolomeo and Brad Rzyczycki. I know I missed a number of past teammates, but I thank you all very much. I want to say a special thanks to every single offensive lineman that I ever played behind. Thank you for blocking for me. There was no me without you guys.

I want to thank all of the hundreds of athletes that I played against throughout my career. You all made me a better person and a more competitive athlete. You all pushed me to give my best effort day in and day out and for that I want to say I appreciate you all.

I want to give special thanks to Mercyhurst Prep and Mercyhurst University for allowing me to be a part of your educational communities. I owe much of my success to the education that I received from both institutions. Thank you for always believing in me.

Dr. William Garvey, thank you for giving me the opportunity to experience Higher Education on such a demanding level like the standards that Mercyhurst University still upholds. Without our meeting, my success may never have happened. Thank you for inspiring me to be the best that I could be and for making education a higher priority than Football.

I want to say thank you to my three sons for making me that happiest father in the entire world. Thank you all for being such good kids. Dante' you are the oldest and your younger brothers will always look up to you. Thank you for learning constantly and staying by my side. Chrissy and I love you very much. Jordan I want to thank you for your wonderful personality and I want you to know how much Chrissy and I love you. We will always be here for you no matter what. Craig Jr. thank you for being such a great baby. You have brought true love to my life and you put a smile on my face every time I see you. Keep beating the challenges that you face and that you will continue to face as life passes you by. Your Mom and I will always be here to support you. We love you with all of our hearts.

I would like to acknowledge a good friend of mine who became my mentor as I entered my professional career. Mike Ruzzi, thank you for all you have done for me. You took me in right out of college raw as could be and molded me into your Co-Anchor. We had a nice run my friend and we built a special bond. You taught me that family is the most important thing in this world. Money and fame will come and go, but your family will always be there. I loved the relationship between you and your father and I appreciate the bond that you have with your Mom. You are a good Son, a good Uncle and someone I'm honored to call my brother.

I would like to thank Kirk Shields and Brenda Harrell for taking a chance on me at Springleaf Financial Services. You both are great people who motivates and cares about your employees. You are straight shooters and I have learned so much from both of you on a business standpoint. Thank you for believing in me and always being there to give me the advice that I needed. I also want to thank my staff and friends at Springleaf for encouraging me. Thank you Paul Stickrath, Brad Marshall, Lisa Langford, Vicki Bozian, John Brownell, Lee Comegys, Angela Geraghty, Brittney Keith, Otie Thompson, Deborah Andrews, Michael Martinez, Craig Faircloth and Angela Wood. Special thanks to Carol Jameson and all upper management at Springleaf Financial.

Even though these guys were my teammates and were mentioned before, I wanted to give a special thanks to a few of my close friends. Khyl Horton I want to thank you for pushing me to be great and keeping my story alive. Thank you for being a true friend and loving me like a brother. I want to say thank you to my good friend Jeff Sansom who is no longer with us. He made me a better person and he was the calm that I needed in irate situations. I love his family dearly, Melvan and Stella Sansom are like second parents to me and I thank my big brother Donnie Sansom for always being there for me and my kids. When Jeff passed away, a little bit of me left with him. I miss my brother every single day. Freddie Jones, I thank you for being a motivator. I appreciate all of the times you lifted me up and gave me your true advice. I have mad love for you bro. I also want to thank my best friend Otha Davidson. We have been through it all bro. Through the thick and the thin. I want to thank you for telling me the truth 100% of the time and for not being a yes man. I know I can always count on you to shoot it straight with me. I have three boys and you have three girls and we always have said that your kids are my nieces and my kids are your nephews. We have a tight bond that will never be broken and I want to say thank you for all you have ever done for me. Much love my brotha!

I'd like to also thank to my 12th Grade English Teacher Kathy Pirello. Mrs. Pirello I never forgot what you said to me nearly 20 years ago. You gave me the courage and inspiration to write this Autobiography. I thank you from the bottom of my heart. I want to thank all of the staff at American Star Publishing for taking a chance on me and my book. You will never be forgotten.

Last and definitely not least, I would like to thank my parents. Thank you for having me and for both taking part in raising me separately. I take different stages of my life and I put them together to get a complete childhood experience. You both were different, but great parents. We all have flaws and I'm sure you'll agree you both have flaws as well, but the one thing I admire about you both is how you have admitted your mistakes and have worked to build a special relationship with me now that I'm an adult. It's truly special and I adore our relationships. I love you both with the bottom of my heart and I want to say thank you for not only inspiring me to write this book, but for bouncing different ideas off of me which challenged my way of thinking. Thank you for letting me share a portion of your adult lives with the readers. Without them knowing about you both, they truly wouldn't be able to learn everything about me. Thank you and I love you both!

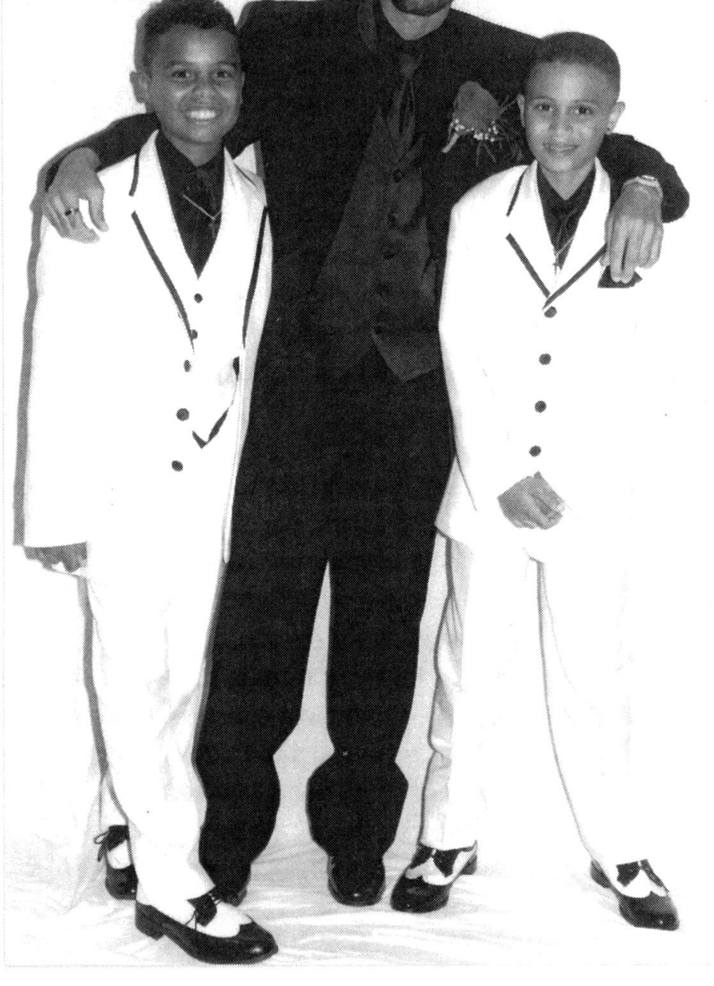

Dedication

My book is dedicated to one of my best friends, Jeffrey Wayne Sansom, who passed away on February 8, 2013. He was an actor, playwright, freelance editor, videographer and was the Godfather to our two oldest children Dante' and Jordan Woodard. Jeff would light up the room when he entered and his positive attitude was contagious. Jeff would be proud of me for writing about my life for the simple fact that he knew how I love to inspire others. He did the same when he was with us. I thank you Jeff for being such a great person, a friend that I could call my brother and an incredible human being. You are gone, but not forgotten. That's why this book is dedicated to you! I'll love you always bro!